WOMEN'S ROLE IN COUNTERING TERRORISM

HEARING

BEFORE THE

SUBCOMMITTEE ON TERRORISM, NONPROLIFERATION, AND TRADE

OF THE

COMMITTEE ON FOREIGN AFFAIRS
HOUSE OF REPRESENTATIVES

ONE HUNDRED FIFTEENTH CONGRESS

SECOND SESSION

FEBRUARY 27, 2018

Serial No. 115–111

Printed for the use of the Committee on Foreign Affairs

Available via the World Wide Web: http://www.foreignaffairs.house.gov/ or
http://www.gpo.gov/fdsys/

U.S. GOVERNMENT PUBLISHING OFFICE

28–824PDF   WASHINGTON : 2018

CONTENTS

Page

WITNESSES

LETTERS, STATEMENTS, ETC., SUBMITTED FOR THE HEARING

APPENDIX

WOMEN'S ROLE IN COUNTERING TERRORISM

TUESDAY, FEBRUARY 27, 2018

HOUSE OF REPRESENTATIVES,
SUBCOMMITTEE ON TERRORISM, NONPROLIFERATION, AND TRADE,
COMMITTEE ON FOREIGN AFFAIRS,
Washington, DC.

The subcommittee met, pursuant to notice, at 2:00 p.m., in room 2172 Rayburn House Office Building, Hon. Ted Poe (chairman of the subcommittee) presiding.

Mr. POE. The subcommittee will come to order.

Without objection, all members may have 5 days to submit statements and questions, extraneous materials for the record subject to the length limitation in the rules. I recognize myself for an opening statement.

The spread of terrorism and extremist ideas has claimed countless lives, destroyed hundreds of communities and spawned radical groups around the world. Women in particular have long been the victims of these radical ideas.

Just last week, the terrorist group Boko Haram targeted a girls' school in Nigeria and abducted more than 100 young girls. This incident follows the 2014 abduction of 270 Nigerian school girls of which 112 are still missing.

These acts are far from uncommon among Islamic terrorist organizations. Across the world, jihadist networks subject women and young girls to horrendous human rights violations.

These male-dominated extremist groups frequently deny basic rights like access to education or political representation to women as a core component of their ideas.

Terrorist groups like ISIS and Boko Haram are often the worst abusers of women, forcing them into marriages and sexual slavery. It should be no surprise that the status of women in a society is often an important indicator as to how vulnerable it is to violence and radicalization.

Yet, while being one of the primary targets of terrorist groups, women are also being radicalized and recruited into these groups. Some support the group's operations, enforce its laws, or marry, and bear children of terrorist fighters. Others actually commit these acts of terror.

In recent years as many as 3,000 women have traveled to the Middle East to join ISIS with many becoming female suicide bombers.

Despite the marginalization and brutality of women in extremist-held lands, repressive regimes, persistent conflict, and poor devel-

(1)

opment policies sometimes create conditions that make groups like ISIS to be seen as an opportunity for women.

Once radicalized, terrorist organizations will leverage the status of women to further their violent goals. For example, Boko Haram has exploited cultural perceptions of women in Nigeria as nonviolent and unlikely to be involved in terrorism, to use them as intelligence and recruiting tools.

In our effort to combat terrorism and extremism abroad, we have neglected the important role of women and how they can play a part in actually preventing radicalization and facilitating peace building in areas long worn by violence.

Women are well placed in homes, schools, and communities to challenge extremist narratives. Research shows that antiterrorism messages can be more effectively spread by women because they are more directly involved with those most vulnerable to the terrorist recruitment of the world's youth.

Given their importance in families and communities, it's essential that women both at home and abroad are more meaningfully enlisted in the fight against terrorism.

Two years ago, as French police hunted for the mastermind behind the Paris attacks that killed 130, it was a woman who reported the whereabouts to the police.

Her role as a surrogate mother to family members of the attacker allowed her access and trust that men unfamiliar to the family would have never gained.

Her brave action prevented a planned follow-on attack. Examples such as this demonstrate the crucial role of women in spotting emerging violence and gaining trust within families and communities.

Unfortunately, we often lack their perspectives because women are underrepresented in governments where terrorist groups are most active.

Because of their better ability to build trust, women have proven to improve the outcomes of conflict mediation and peace building. A study of 40 peace processes in 35 countries over the past 30 years found that when women were involved, more agreements were reached, implemented, and sustained.

As more and more terrorist groups threaten our country, our allies, and our interests, it is vital that we leverage the talents and perspectives of women as part of a bigger approach to ensure security at home and abroad.

It must be the policy of the United States that as we work in societies damaged by years of war and political unrest we empower women to have a larger voice.

In this fight against terrorism, we need everybody at the table, especially women. And I will yield to the gentleman from Massachusetts, the ranking member, Mr. Keating, for his opening statements.

Mr. KEATING. Thank you, Chairman Poe. I would like to thank our panel for joining us on this very important topic.

Quite frankly, in 2001 no one imagined how much the threat of terrorism would, indeed, change. The days of countering terrorism through undermining and eliminating self-contained organizations is over.

Despite many successes, we often feel like we are playing a rigged game of Whac-A-Mole and all the while the organized groups like al-Qaeda or Boko Haram continue to survive and evolve as ever present and legitimate threats to the United States and our allies.

Our security agencies here in the United States and those of our allies have been working tirelessly to adapt to a changing landscape, and as we have come to understand the new terrorist threats we face in foreign fighters and lone wolves, and the often unpredictable radicalization of vulnerable individuals in our communities, fortunately we have the ability to learn more about these new approaches and new actors who are critical to the fight against terrorism, and actors who really should have been a part of the strategy all along.

Civil society, the rule of law, and the focus of our hearing this afternoon—women—are integral to our success in countering the terrorist threats we face today.

By consistently failing to meaningfully engage women in combating terrorism and extremism, we are failing to not only address part of the problem but we are failing to pursue a whole new range of solutions.

Our mission is to be most effective and efficient in keeping Americans and our allies safe from terrorism and to have this exclusion continue or not to maximize this important resource is unacceptable.

Roughly half the world is made up of women. Half the victims of terrorism are women. In communities struggling to rebuild and achieve security and stability again after a terrorist threat has finally been temporarily kept at bay, roughly half the people in that community will be women.

And yet, when we look at the breakdown of who is empowered to have a meaningful role in combating terrorism, women are severely under-represented. At a time when resources are tight, when we can't seem to have a single sustained success story of eliminating a terrorist threat anywhere, and when instead the problem might be growing, why are we tying one of our hands behind our back?

When we think about radicalization and terrorism, there are always warning signs. A parent notices her child's behavior, notices whether there has been a recent change in that behavior.

A teacher notices one of her students has been increasingly withdrawn in class. They change their appearance or their opinions have started to become more extreme.

Often, women are on the front lines of noticing these warnings signs associated with radicalization. What resources do they have when they are faced with a situation?

Far too often, women don't know or trust who they can go to with that information or, worse yet, when some of them brought their concerns to law enforcement, they are ignored.

Fortunately, this has been changing, thanks to the incredible strength and determination of countless women around the world as well as many men who early on understood the importance of supporting these women in their mission.

Thanks to them, we finally started to move in the right direction. Congress passed the Women, Peace, and Security Act last fall, which will require a strategy be in place to promote the participation of women in U.S. foreign policy.

More research has been done to show the benefits achieved when women have a seat at the table and more women than ever before have been able to join the ranks of their male counterparts in the security sector and in leadership posts where they have a real role in fighting terrorism and shaping peaceful resolutions to conflict.

We still have a very long way to go, however, and the threats we face from terrorism are not going to sit patient while we get there. The whole of government approach does not mean listening to and working with just half the resources we have available to us in tackling these threats.

I, therefore, look forward to hearing our witnesses today. I hope that we can discuss lessons learned so far, the gaps that still remain, and including women alongside men in efforts to combat terrorism, and what we can do about it, what we should be doing in terms of our foreign assistance, our military assistance, our diplomatic missions, and our intelligence missions.

What must men start doing differently and what changes do we need to start making things happen now so that our counterterrorism strategy is no longer just half of what it could be?

I yield back.

Mr. POE. I thank the gentleman from Massachusetts.

And without objection, the chair will recognize the gentle lady from Florida, Ms. Frankel, for an opening statement.

Ms. FRANKEL. Thank you, Mr. Poe and Mr. Keating, for convening this meeting.

For too long, women's diverse roles in countering and supporting violent extremism has been overlooked and it just needs more attention. I am glad we are doing that today and I thank you, all of you, for being here.

Ignoring half of the population in the fight against radicalism leaves us with a strategic blind spot and when it comes to violent extremism women can be victims, preventers, and perpetrators.

You know, terrorists do not succumb their victims only with bullets and bombs, as we know. Rape, trafficking, and abuse of women have become all too common weapons of war.

Women are often the first targets of terrorist organizations. ISIS has abducted and raped thousands of women and girls and even used income generated from human trafficking to fill their coffers.

In Nigeria, Boko Haram has kidnapped hundreds of girls and subjected them to countless horrors. Last week, another 110 girls went missing from a group that attacked another school.

The Taliban have attacked girls in Afghanistan, in Pakistan—like we heard about that wonderful young girl, Malala—simply for trying to get an education.

And, sadly, women are not always the innocent. They also support and engage in terrorism. In sub-Saharan Africa, three out of four child suicide bombers are girls and 18 percent of all suicide bombers are women, and I am sure there is a lot of complicated reasons for that that hopefully some of you will address.

When the former wife of a Boko Haram commander was asked why she willingly joined the group, she said they offered her more money, power, and protection than what she was getting within her own community.

Recent research has shed light on factors that lead women to be recruited into terrorist organizations: False promises of protection, escape from an abusive home, and leadership opportunities.

But we still have a limited understanding of what's driving these women in the wrong direction. And as mentioned by my colleagues, women can be and should be on the front lines of countering terrorism, and are uniquely situated to detect early signs of radicalization in youth, especially as mothers.

And whatever—many times their warnings are disregarded and we have to figure out ways to empower them and I hope we will hear some suggestions on that.

I have lots of questions but I am going to wait until it's my turn to ask and, again, I thank you all for being here on this very important subject.

Mr. POE. The gentle lady yields back her time.

I now will recognize each of the witnesses and I would advise all of you that your statements are prepared—your prepared statements are a part of the record and try to keep your statements to no more than 5 minutes and then each member of the panel or each member of the committee will ask you questions.

Dr. Valerie Hudson is professor at the George H. W. Bush School of Government and also is the chair of the Department of International Affairs at the Bush School of Government at Texas A&M University where she directs the program of Women, Peace, and Security. She previously taught at Brigham Young, Northwestern, and Rutgers Universities.

Mr. Haras Rafiq is CEO of Quilliam International. He is currently a member of the United Kingdom's Prime Minister's Community Engagement Forum Task Force and was formerly a member of the U.K. government's task force looking at countering extremism in response to the 2005 terrorist bombings in London.

Ms. Farhat Popal serves as the manager of the Women's Initiative Fellowship and the Afghan Women's Project at the George W. Bush Institute at SMU, not to be confused with the Texas A&M Institution where your cohort, Dr. Hudson, works.

Previously, she worked at the State Department's Bureau of Democracy, Human Rights, and Labor, and as special inspector general for Afghanistan reconstruction.

And Ms. Jamille Bigio is a senior fellow at the Women and Foreign Policy program at the Council on Foreign Relations. Previously, she has served as director of human rights and gender on the White House National Security Council staff.

Dr. Hudson, we will start with you and you have 5 minutes. When that red light comes on, that means you're supposed to stop.

Ms. HUDSON. I'll do my best.

Mr. POE. If you see it.

Ms. HUDSON. Thank you so much.

Mr. POE. In case you were wondering what that meant.

STATEMENT OF VALERIE M. HUDSON, PH.D., PROFESSOR AND GEORGE H.W. BUSH CHAIR, THE BUSH SCHOOL OF GOVERNMENT AND PUBLIC SERVICE, TEXAS A&M UNIVERSITY

Ms. HUDSON. I am grateful to be here today. Thank you so much for inviting me. I hope my short remarks on the linkages between male-female relations, radicalization, and terrorism may be of use to you.

My research team at the Women's Stats Project has been examining the relationship between gender and equality, marriage market obstruction, on the one hand, and the security and stability of nation states on the other for some time now.

This research is most recently funded by the Minerva Initiative of the U.S. Department of Defense. In our efforts, we have concentrated on women's personal empowerment, or disempowerment, at the household level rather than examining broader indicators such as female literacy, female labor force participation, or female parliamentary representation.

Rather, we examine things that are closer to home for women such as property and inheritance rights, rights in marriage, rights in divorce and custody, level of violence against women in the home—in total, 11 such indicators of women's empowerment or disempowerment at the household level.

Then, using large and multi varied modeling measure techniques, we found that this disempowerment—household disempowerment measure is strongly significantly related to multiple measures of political instability, autocracy, lack of freedom, corruption, and internal conflict in the state.

In fact, the overall best predictor of state stability and security was not our control variables such as how urbanized the society was, how fractionalized the society was, colonial status, and several others, but rather women's disempowerment at the household level was the most predictive variable.

Why would there be such a strong and significant association? We argue that the character of male-female relations at the household level is, if you will, the first political order within any human society and this order shapes the development of the nation state in indelible ways.

If the household is an autocracy where men rule over those who are different from them—women—if men feel they have the right to use physical force against those who are different from them—women—if men feel entitled to greater access to household resources than those who are different from them—women—this is the template that will be applied to all who are deemed different in the larger society.

This explains why Elin Bjarnegard and her co-authors have found that men holding deeply gender unequal beliefs also hold far more hostile attitudes toward minority and foreign nations and are significantly more likely to be involved in committing political violence.

How women are treated by men becomes, if you will, a boot camp training men in the arts of violent and exploitative autocracy.

Does the boot camp hypothesis hold for terrorism as well? Yes, it does. Again, using the same techniques, we found every measure of terrorism we examined such as the political terrorist scale, terrorism impact score, terrorism fatalities was strongly, significantly associated with women's personal disempowerment at the household level.

Train men to terrorize women and you train them in terrorism. Relatedly, this also helps explain why the overwhelming majority of mass shooters in the U.S. have histories of domestic violence.

We also undertook the second angle of investigation into the links to terrorism. We examined nations' comparative rates of production of foreign fighters going to fight for ISIS.

Adjusting for total population size, which nations are producing more or less of these foreign fighters? Using data from the Soufan Group on estimated numbers from each country, again, a strong and significant relationship between the national production rate of foreign fighters and our measure of women's personal disempowerment at the household level.

This is the second corroboration of the boot camp hypothesis and I'd like to note this particular research was conducted by my graduate Capstone research team at the Bush School of Government and Public Service for the Office of Global Women's Issues at the State Department.

There are also additional ways. By creating structural instabilities—well, you talked about Boko Haram. Well, one of the structural instabilities is bride price—the price that a groom must pay to a bride's father to marry.

Bride price is subject to extreme inflation and bubbles over time, and this means that young men are priced out of the marriage market.

Boko Haram kidnaps these girls so that young men without bride prices may marry. In a like manner, polygyny and sex ratio alteration also create chronic instability within the system, goading young men into grievance and political terrorism.

In conclusion then, by providing a training course in terrorism, creating structural instability within a society, and disempowering the very voices that might be most persuasive arguing against terrorism—women—the character of male-female relations is a strong determinant of the horizon for peace and security within the society.

Thank you very much.

[The prepared statement of Ms. Hudson follows:]

Valerie M. Hudson, Ph.D.
Professor and George H.W. Bush Chair
Director, Program on Women, Peace, and Security
Department of International Affairs
The Bush School of Government and Public Service
Texas A&M University

The House Committee on Foreign Affairs
Subcommittee on Terrorism, Nonproliferation, and Trade
Hearings on "Women's Role in Countering Terrorism"
27 February 2018

STATEMENT:

Honored members of the House Foreign Affairs Committee, I am delighted to be with you today. I hope my short remarks on the linkages between male/female relations, radicalization, and terrorism may be of use to you.

My research team at The WomanStats Project (http://womanstats.org) has been examining the relationship between gender inequality and marriage market obstruction on the one hand, and the security and stability of nation-states on the other, for some time now. This research is most recently funded by the Minerva Initiative of the US Department of Defense.

In our efforts, we have concentrated on women's personal empowerment or disempowerment at the household level, rather than examining broader indicators such as female literacy, female laborforce participation, or female representation in parliaments. Rather, we examine things closer to home, such as property and inheritance rights, rights in marriage, rights in divorce and custody, level of violence against women in the home--in total eleven such indicators of women's empowerment at the household level. Then, using large-N multivariate modeling techniques, we found that this measure is strongly and significantly related to multiple measures of political instability, autocracy, lack of freedoms, corruption and internal conflict. In fact, the overall best predictor of state stability was not our control variables, such as urbanization, ethnic fractionalization, former colonial status, and several others, but rather women's empowerment at the household level. [1]

Why would there be such a strong and significant association? We argue that the character of male/female relations at the household level is the first political order created within any human society, and that this order shapes the development of the nation-state in indelible ways. If the household is an autocracy where men rule over those who are different from them—women; if men feel they have the right to use physical force against those who are different from them—women; if men feel entitled to greater access to household resources than those who are different from them—women; this is the template that will be applied to *all* who are deemed different in the larger society. This explains why Elin Bjarnegard and her co-authors have found that men holding deeply gender unequal beliefs also hold far more hostile attitudes towards minorities and foreign nations—and are also more likely to be involved in committing political violence. [2, 3] How women are treated by men becomes a boot camp, if you will, training men in the arts of violent and exploitative autocracy.

Does the boot camp hypothesis hold for terrorism, as well? Yes, it does. Again using large-N multivariate modeling, we found that every measure of terrorism we examined, including the Political Terror Scale, the Terrorism Impact Score, and

Terrorism Fatalities, was strongly and significantly associated with women's personal disempowerment at the household level. Train men to terrorize women, and you train them in terrorism. Relatedly, this also helps explain why the overwhelming majority of mass shooters in the United States have histories of domestic violence. [4]

We also undertook a second angle of investigation into the links to terrorism, and examined nations' comparative rate of production of foreign fighters going to ISIS-controlled territory over the last few years. That is, adjusting for their total population size, which nations were producing more (or less) of these foreign fighters? Using data from the Soufan Group on estimated numbers of foreign fighters from each country, we found a very strong and significant relationship between the national production rate of foreign fighters and our measure of women's personal disempowerment at the household level. This is a second corroboration of the boot camp hypothesis, and I'd like to note that this particular research was conducted by my graduate capstone research team at the Bush School of Government and Public Service for the Office of Global Women's Issues at the US State Department.

There is an additional way in which the societal structure of male/female relations affects the level of terrorist and rebel activity within the society, and that is through providing goads that make the recruitment of young men by terrorist and rebel groups very easy. For example, about 75% of the world's population lives in societies in which marriage involves a substantial payment, and most of the time that takes the form of brideprice, where the groom must pay the bride's father. This often involves a large sum of money or assets—usually several times the annual income of the family. Brideprice is subject to often dramatic inflation, much like real estate bubbles, and such inflation prices many young men out of the marriage market altogether. Terrorist and rebel groups become aware of the ensuing grievance, and will offer to pay brideprice on behalf of young men who would otherwise not be able to marry. In a recent article, Hilary Matfess and I explore this phenomenon, and find that many groups use brideprice to attract recruits, such as Boko Haram, Lashkar-e-Taiba, ISIS, Hezbollah, and many others. Some governments, such as the Saudi government, understand this linkage and try to put legal caps on brideprice, as well as pay brideprice for their most vulnerable young men. [5]

Remembering that brideprice is part of that first political order that subordinates and "others" women within their own households, we see that in addition to being a boot camp for terror, this first political order can also produce goads for young men to join terrorist and rebel groups. That is, the marriage market becomes chronically obstructed as a result of that subordinative order. Polygyny also serves the same type of goading function; for example, recruitment of young men into terrorist and rebel groups in West Africa has been linked by researchers to areas of more prevalent polygyny, for polygyny also obstructs the marriage market for young men. [6] In similar fashion, sex ratio alterations, in which girls are culled from the population through sex-selective abortion and female infanticide, can likewise produce outcomes in which tens of millions of women go missing, similarly obstructing marriage markets due to the scarcity of women. [7] Lest you feel this is an issue only in China and India, there are now 19 nations with seriously abnormal birth sex ratios, including countries such as Armenia, Albania, and Azerbaijan. [8] When you subordinate women at the household level, as brideprice, polygyny, and sex ratio alteration all do, societies become *structurally* unstable, and the link to terror and rebellion become clear.

In conclusion, by providing a training course in terrorism as well as creating structural instability within a society, the character of male/female relations is a strong determinant of the horizon for peace and security within a society. This means that gender equality is thus a hard security issue, and is recognized as such by this Congress through its passage of the Women, Peace, and Security Act of 2017. As a former Secretary of State put it in 2012, "The subjugation of women is a threat to the common security of our world and to the national security of our country." [9]

Thank you so much for your invitation to address this subcommittee.

References

[1] Hudson, Valerie M., Donna Lee Bowen, Perpetua Lynne Nielsen, *The First Political Order: Sex, Governance, and National Security*, forthcoming

[2] Bjarnegard, Elin, Erik Melander (2017) "Pacific Men: How the Feminist Gap Explains Hostility," The Pacific Review, DOI: 10.1080/09512748.2016.1264456

[3] Bjarnegard, Elin, Karen Brouneus, Erik Melander (2017) "Honor and Political Violence: Micro-Level Findings from a Survey in Thailand," *Journal of Peace Research*, 546(6), 748-761.

[4] Hudson, Valerie M. and Patrticia Leidl (2018) "Did It Mean Nothing?" Columbia University Press Blog, 20 February, http://www.cupblog.org/2018/02/20/did-it-mean-nothing/

[5] Hudson, Valerie M. and Hilary Matfess (2017) "In Plain Sight: The Neglected Linkage Between Brideprice, Raiding, and Rebellion," *International Security*, Vol. 42, No. 1 (Summer 2017), pp. 7–40, doi:10.1162/ISEC_a_00289

[6] Mokuwa, Esther, Maarten Voors, Erwin Bulte and Paul Richards (2011) "Peasant Grievance and Insurgency in Sierra Leone: Judicial Serfdom as a Driver of Conflict." *African Affairs* 110, no. 440 (2011): 339-366.

[7] Hudson, Valerie and Andrea Den Boer (2004) *Bare Branches: The Security Implications of Asia 's Surplus Male Population*, Cambridge, MA: MIT Press.

[8] Hudson, Valerie M. and Andrea M. Den Boer (2015) "When a Boy's Life is Worth More Than His Sister's," *Foreign Policy*, July 30, http://foreignpolicy.com/2015/07/30/when-a-boys-life-is-worth-more-than-his-sisters-sex-ratio/

[9] Hudson, Valerie M. and Patricial Leidl (2015) *The Hillary Doctrine: How Sex Came to Matter in American Foreign Policy*, New York: Columbia University Press.

Mr. POE. Thank you, Dr. Hudson.

Mr. Rafiq, thank you for being here. Thank you for coming across the pond, so to speak, to be here to testify at this hearing. We appreciate it very much.

You may proceed with your testimony.

STATEMENT OF MR. HARAS RAFIQ, CHIEF EXECUTIVE OFFICER, QUILLIAM INTERNATIONAL

Mr. RAFIQ. Thank you, Chairman Poe, Ranking Member Keating, and Member Frankel for inviting me to travel across the pond and speak on this very important subject.

My colleague—my executive director at Quilliam U.S. would have been here but he's in Nigeria right now training male and female members of civil society on critical thinking to tackle terrorism.

Quilliam is an organization that operates in three countries—the U.K., U.S., and Canada—and it's an organization that was set up by former extremists to challenge Islamist terrorism and Islamist ideology.

I think it's very important that we use the correct terminology and we use Islamism and differentiate between Islam, because just as there's a difference between the word social and socialism, there is a difference between Islam, which is a religion that's practiced by Muslims around the world in many different ways.

Islamism is a distinct political ideology when merged with certain Salafi Wahhabi theology is one interpretation and is part of a civil war that's going on within Islam right now.

Chairman Poe, you're absolutely right that women are ideally placed to be primary and secondary intervention providers because of their proximity, their prestige, and their passion.

They are much more effective than any government initiatives direct or any governments can be and quite often are more effective than men when it comes to providing these interventions for young male and female members of their families.

In order to understand and the best way to actually look at projects to prevent terrorism—we need to look at the radicalization process and there are four key aspects to it.

The first one, there has to be a grievance, whether it's genuine, partial, or perceived. The second one, there has to be a charismatic recruiter or recruiters that will recruit people who have these grievances.

The third thing is there has to be an identity crisis. People have to be told that the only way they're going to find solutions is if they join a particular Islamist gang, and the fourth one is the ideology of Islamism itself that actually provides solutions for some of these people.

In the case of women and our ground-breaking research, which I co-authored, called "Caliphates: Women and the Appeal of Islamic States," the four main solutions for women were the following—the first one, the promise of empowerment; the second one, the promise of deliverance; the third one, the promise of participation; and the fourth one, the promise of piety.

Once we understand these processes, we can start looking at projects on ways of actually preventing terrorism, and I just want to touch very briefly on four projects that we've worked on—or that we've run—and you can read more about them in the written testimony.

The first one is the current project in Nigeria, which is around critical thinking, which our—my executive director, Mohammed Rahim, is delivering right now. It's on critical thinking.

The second one is AMATE, which is the American Muslims Against Terrorism and Extremism. We run that with our partners in the U.S., Masjid Muhammad and also with Greene Street Communications, and in fact the project is led by an African-American Muslim woman, Jamilah Fraser.

And since its launch on January the 8th of this year, we've reached 705,000 people out of which 65,000—sorry, 86,000 people have been women, and I can go into the demographics a little bit more.

The third one is the rehabilitation of former terrorists within the U.K. There have been a number of people that have been released here in the U.S. over the last 12 months and we've worked with some of them, male and female, and there will be some news and some announcements that we'll have where we've de-radicalized, used models that we've used in other countries to de-radicalize individuals here in the U.S. And by the way, there are just under 20 further people that we—convicted terrorists in the U.S. that we release within the next 12 months.

The fourth one is FATE, which is Families Against Terrorism and Extremism, and that's one of our flagship programs where we've operated in 22 countries with 115 organizations.

Ten thousand providers of services have been the beneficiary of training. We've up-scaled—we've trained people in North Africa and in central Europe as well, and again, we've helped them build messages and really used women and families to actually become this bulwark against terrorism.

There are about 12 recommendations in my testimony but the gist, really, of the recommendations are around the following.

At this moment in time, we are actually playing Whac-A-Mole. We are actually focusing on a strategy that is about terrorism prevention, and once we actually contain one global jihadist terrorist threat, there is a new one that pops up.

But ISIS and al-Qaeda didn't breed extremism. Extremism bred them. In order to actually become more effective, we have to recognize that there is a global jihadist insurgency and we also need an effective counter extremism strategy which actually works with women, empowers women, and empowers civil society as a whole to take on this challenge and counter the narratives that would radicalize our youngsters.

Thank you.

[The prepared statement of Mr. Rafiq follows:]

Challenging Extremism | Promoting Pluralism | Inspiring Change

UK - OFFICE 109, 4 LITTLE PORTLAND STREET, LONDON W1W 7JB, UK | T +44 207 182 7283 | www.quilliaminternational.com
USA - 535 ANTON PARKWAY, SUITE 1125, COSTA MESA, CA 92626 | T +1 202 577 5695 | www.quilliaminternational.com

<u>*CONGRESSIONAL TESTIMONY*</u>

The Role of Women in Countering Violent Extremism

Testimony before
Terrorism, Non-Proliferation, and Trade Subcommittee

Committee on Foreign Affairs

United States House of Representatives

27th February 2018

Haras Rafiq
Chief Executive Officer
Quilliam International

I wish to thank Chairman Poe, Ranking Member Keating, and the other Members of
the Subcommittee for the opportunity to discuss the role of women in Countering Violent
Extremism.

My name is Haras Rafiq and I am the Chief Executive Officer of Quilliam International.
Quilliam is the world's first counter-extremism organisation and aims to challenge extremist
narratives while advocating pluralistic, democratic alternatives that are consistent with
universal human rights. Quilliam has a full spectrum and values-based approach to counter-
extremism which means promoting pluralism and inspiring change.

To pursue our work more effectively and ensure that we are localising our efforts. We are
currently operating in the UK, USA and Canada as well as a Global team for projects around
the world.

Challenging extremism is the duty of all responsible members of society. Not least because
cultural insularity and extremism are products of the failures of wider society to foster a
shared sense of belonging and to advance liberal democratic values.

Quilliam seeks to challenge what we think, and the way we think. We aim to generate
creative, informed and inclusive discussions to counter the ideological underpinnings of
terrorism, while simultaneously providing evidence-based policy recommendations to
governments and building civil society networks and programmes to lead the change
towards a more positive future.

Background and Rational for Empowering Women in CVE

Current strategies for tackling violent extremism –have a fundamental blind spot. This blind spot is the way in which civil society is underutilised to act as primary and secondary intervention providers to prevent the process of radicalisation to violent extremism and hence terrorism

Families and hence women are the best placed to counter violent extremism because they meet the 3 P's that we look for:

Proximity, Prestige and Passion.

Proximity: families are close to individuals vulnerable to radicalisation and recruitment to violent extremism. Having identified vulnerable individuals through target audience analysis, families are ideally placed to intervene because of their Proximity to them.

Prestige: families have credibility as intervention providers that many other stakeholders lack and we know that reducing the role of the state in CVE and de-securitising this area is important for effective interventions. Because of their Prestige, families are much better placed to intervene effectively, as safe guarders, intervention providers, and messengers in counter speech.

Passion: families are uniquely placed to communicate emotionally to protect their loved ones from the social harms of violent extremism, and the security threats of terrorism. Whereas many stakeholders can only respond to extremism with logic and counters to violent extremism, families can respond with Passion, which is both a more effective counter to violent extremism, and a credible alternative

Violent Extremism and the Appeal of Groups such as ISIS and Al-Qaeda

The most recent Jihadist phenomenon that the world has witnessed has been ISIS and their claim to a utopian Islamic State. Although, ISIS has been militarily defeated for now, it would be a mistake to believe that the underpinning ideology of Islamist Jihadism has been defeated. It would also be a mistake to just focus on the ISIS brand as extremism in isolation as groups such as ISIS, AL Qaeda, Boko Haram, Al Shabab et al did not inspire extremism; extremism inspired them.

To establish terms up front, we make a clear difference between Islam and Islamism. Islam is a religion practiced by 1.5 billion Muslims, whose clear majority are non-violent and peaceful, but on the flip side of the coin, have been the victims of extremist brutality, barbarism and draconian tactics. We describe Islamism as a political ideology that seeks to impose any interpretation of Islam as State Law usually in the form to oppress, restrict and retard growth

Islamist extremism and the radicalization to violence relies on the following four factors being present

- The first, is a sense of grievance, whether real or perceived, that gives rise to anger and despair in some cases but more than that it begins the desire to seek out an alternative solution to and individuals' problem
- The second is an identity crisis that is born from that sense of grievance. So, for example, if the sense of grievance was the Bosnia genocide, as it was for many in the past, then the identity crisis born from it, is to question whether one really belongs in the society that they live in.
- The third factor is the presence of charismatic extremist recruiters, who provide a sense of belonging, where perhaps that sense of grievance, and the identity crisis, led to a vacuum in belonging. He or she steps in where family should be stepping in, where a father figure should be stepping in, or mother figure, and provides that sense of belonging.
- The fourth, is the ideology. In this case, the Islamist ideology, that is then peddled as the solution to that sense of grievance, the solution to the identity crisis, and the ideal that the charismatic recruiter says that he or she are adhering to themselves.

The above is designed to move the individual through various stages of an identity that believes that all who do not belong to their world view are the other, are all the same, are all oppressing them, are all collectively guilty (hence no innocents), do not fit into their supremacism narrative and that self-defense and violence need to eventually be applied against them.

Women Radicalized to join ISIS from Western Countries

Our ground-breaking report Caliphettes: Women and the Appeal of Islamic State[1], examined the appeal of the Islamic Sate "caliphate" to women. To do this, we embarked upon a close analysis of Islamic State's official propaganda and unofficial proselytisers. In the process, four promises – empowerment, deliverance, participation and piety – are identified as the organisation's key pull factors.

- The promise of empowerment conveyed by Islamic State's official and unofficial propaganda encourages women to understand joining the organisation to reverse the ills that they face in life outside the "caliphate". By joining Islamic State, the line goes, women can defiantly take charge of their lives in the same way that men can: through living in Islamic State's "caliphate" and supporting its jihad by marrying a fighter, women are led to believe that they can emancipate themselves from *kufr* (disbelief).

- The deliverance promise focuses on the idea that, by joining Islamic State, grievances that women suffer in the West are immediately resolved. Women can be freed from daily degradations and disbelief and are instead assimilated into a tightknit collective sisterhood that will provide them with a network of support and friendship. Reflective of this, the ideas of redemption and deliverance tend to be directed to females by females.

---

[1] https://www.quilliaminternational.com/shop/e-publications/caliphettes-women-and-the-appeal-of-islamic-state/

- The participation promise incentivizes women to join Islamic State even though their role is strictly non-military. It conveys a sense that there is more to the "caliphate's" jihad than fighting and that, for women, there is a specific state-building role. A constant theme in Islamic State propaganda is that supporting the "caliphate", making it grow and flourish, is the job of everyone. For women, this takes the role of providing, maintaining and educating its" cubs", the next generation of fighters, as well as supporting their soldier spouses.

- The last promise of Islamic State's women-orientated propaganda is piety, something built up the theological imperative to join the group. The alleged pristine nature of an "Islamic existence" in the "caliphate" is a means of justifying each stress and sacrifice and acts as a means for recruiters to exert peer pressure to push others to make *hijra* (migrating).

These four solutions alone did not cause female supporters of Islamic State in the West to make *hijra* and *join ISIS*. However, when combined with the group's copious amounts of audio-visual propaganda, they played a crucial role in the rhetorical armoury of the "caliphate's" charismatic recruiters.

The discussion on the radicalisation of women is overly gendered and, all too often, predicated on misconceptions. In reality, when it comes to joining violent extremist causes, women are susceptible to the very same processes as men: narratives, ideology, grievances, and various push and pull factors. Reflecting this, the last part of this report delivers policy recommendations on how we must reappraise our attempts to counter the twin processes of female radicalisation and recruitment, in line with general counter-radicalisation, but using women as specific entry points.

Programs and Women Involvement

1. Tafakkur Critical Thinking Program

To amplify our point, at present our Executive Director for Quilliam North America, Dr. Muhammad Fraser-Rahim and our Quilliam team is in Nigeria, West Africa where we are incorporating a cutting-edge training called Taffakur.

Taffakur means to think, reflect and ponder in Arabic, is a critical thinking tool in which we are working directly with individuals from conflict zones in Nigeria, including Adamawa, Yobe and Borno States and directly with women.

Workshop Objectives

By the end of the Workshop, participants will be able to:

- Understand the genealogy of terrorism in Africa, the goals and objectives of extremist groups, and the discourse of P/CVE;
- Know Islam's contribution to civilization, it's spread across the world, Islamic philosophy, and experientially understand the concept of Ikhtilaaf (respect for differences of opinions in Islam)

- Think for themselves, via learning about and practicing the Socratic Method via Tafakkur, Circles
- Understand the discourse of service learning, to design tailored P/CVE interventions

2. Ideological Rehabilitation

In the United States, our team has been working with women and men to help them on their exit and journey out of extremism. This one on one engagement requires skilled people who understand the issues facing individuals and communities as they remain vulnerable to both online and person to person recruitment. We continue to build on our work doing this globally and continue to seek to expand throughout the world.

There will be some announcements on the success of this project in the near future

3. AMATE (American Muslims Against Terrorism and Extremism)

- Officially launched – January 8, 2018
- Press release to media
- Online pickups: 129 outlets, potential audience = 134,167,900
- Geotargeting to mobile devices
- Social media outreach (Facebook, Instagram and Twitter)

The AMATE Initiative, American Muslims Against Terrorism & Extremism, launched officially on January 8th of this year and right away it garnered tremendous interest. The effort is anchored by a website complete with resources for those seeking a way out of extremism, those who might be on the path to extremism who know that they've gotten themselves into trouble and even video testimonials from former extremists. The resources are not only targeted to those who have already been radicalized or are on the path to radicalization, but it also targets the loved ones of those who have chosen that very dark path. We know that, often, families look on feeling nearly helpless as they try to bring their loved ones back from the brink. So, it was very important that we provided a solution that they could easily utilize as well.

Since the January 8th launch, the site has reached more than 705,000 individuals through the use of a robust mobile device geotargeting campaign. Close to 400,000 of those are men aged 25-34, nearly 240,000 are men aged 18-24 and close to 60,000 aged 35-44. But, we know that women are often the guiding lights helping to pull young men out of that dark world, so the campaign has also targeted women, leading them to those resources that will help them talk to their loved ones about the dangerous path that they've chosen. Since the campaign launch, more than 86,000 women have been reached with 65,000 of those being in the 25-34 age group, 15,000 aged 18-24 and over 6,000 aged 35-44.

Those numbers are phenomenal, but they could not have been possible without a thoughtful investment of financial resources. To continue this great work, it will take a further investment in order to continue to meet those who would wreck lives and cause havoc in the world where, more and more often we find they hide – on the world wide web.

4. **FATE – Families Against Terrorism and Extremism**

Please see case study below

Case Study – Project FATE (Families Against Terrorism and Extremism)

FATE - Families Against Terrorism and Extremism

Families are often the people most impacted by acts of violent terrorism and recruitment to extremist ideas. They are the first hit with loss and pain after a terrorist act and feel deep pangs of shame and guilt when a loved one becomes radicalized.

Yet, families are not just victims of violent extremism; they are vital partners in peace and their engagement in constructive responses to terrorism and extremism, of all kinds is critical in prevention, and mitigation of the impacts of violence and radicalization on individuals and communities.

Families are educators, guides and helpers. They are protectors and comforters, positioned to intervene if a loved one takes a dangerous path. They are trusted confidants, motivators and an anchor for the next generation. To effectively play their role in protecting their loved ones from radicalization and recovering from acts of terrorism, they need support, opportunities to connect with others in similar situations, training and a platform to share their stories so that the human impact of terrorism and radicalization is understood.

About FATE

Families Against Terrorism and Extremism (FATE) was established in March 2016 by a partnership between Quilliam International and the US State Department division (GEC) to create a support network for civil society organisations (CSOs), state agencies, individuals and communities to come together to share ideas, experiences and resources around protecting and empowering families against terrorism and radicalisation. The US Government initiated the project for one year and have now handed the project over to Quilliam International. The first FATE Summit, held in Paris in March 2016, brought together over 100 CSO representatives and countering violent extremism (CVE) practitioners over two days to explore various themes around the role families can play in protecting their communities against radicalisation and to identify their support needs.

Some of the current participants and network members include The Association of British Muslims, Women Without Borders, Sons and Daughters of the World, The Breck Foundation and Mothers for Life and The Arq Foundation.

Since the Summit, FATE has facilitated online and offline communication, provided support to CSOs and practitioners through creating networking opportunities and resource finding and offered guidance and advice to network members in their work.

With a strong and active network across Europe, FATE was then able to broaden its work in the North Africa region. Convening its second Summit in Tunisia in November 2016, where a further 120 CSO representatives and countering violent extremism (CVE) practitioners over two days to explore various themes around the role families can play in protecting their communities against radicalisation and to identify their support needs. This was followed by online and face-to-face training around 'Building Family Resilience against Terrorism and Radicalisation,' that took place in Morocco and Tunisia, FATE hopes to build a global movement that strengthens family's resilience against the radicalization process and provide them with the support they need when impacted by acts of violent extremism.

In March 2016, Quilliam founded the Families Against Terrorism and Extremism (FATE) Network in Europe. FATE is a countering violent extremism project that aims to empower civil society to generate effective CVE interventions, especially by using with family-oriented themes

FATE's strategy is to:

1) Develop a network of civil society organisations who have direct contact with families

2) Collaborate with this network of organisations and families to create engaging, hyperlocal counter speech content with family-oriented themes

3) Engage this network and use hypertargeting with social media tools to deliver counter speech to our target audience: individuals vulnerable to radicalisation, extremism and terrorism

4) Incorporate calls to action within this counter speech to allow us to identify individuals for online and offline CVE interventions, then use FATE's triage model to identify the right intervention for each individual

5) Build the capacity of the FATE network to provide effective CVE interventions through skills-building workshops (spotting the signs of radicalisation, conducting targeted interventions, developing counter speech, providing direct intervention online or on the phone, and cooperating with authorities), a train-the-trainer model, and the FATE Support Request Form.

6) Empower families in the FATE network to understand radicalisation, extremism, terrorism and how to counter these phenomena so they can play a prevention and intervention role through skills-building workshops, online modules, and as eventual beneficiaries of the train-the-trainer model.

7) Link vulnerable individuals to organisations within the FATE network so they can deliver the right intervention in each case.

8) Monitor the performance of FATE counter speech and its reception among our target audience, with a focus on the success of our calls to actions in providing FATE with individuals for further intervention. Evaluate the skills increase among network organisations and families trained by FATE. Record the individual intervention journeys of beneficiaries within our target audience to ensure high retention rate and track the link between attitudinal shift (online) and behavioural change (offline).

Highlights from Year One

In Year One, FATE has focused on building a brand and growing trust among organisations that are crucial to the successful implementation of its strategy. We have done this by building a fully-interactive website hub for our members that houses our counter speech content, other resources and information about our events, a blog for members to write on and a forum where members can engage with each other, and which will soon be the portal for our online workshop modules. We have a delivered a successful media and social media strategy that has seen over 1 million views of FATE's counter speech videos, 94 articles and stories published, 84,000 engagements through our presence on 5 social media platforms and in 5 languages.

FATE has run international summits in Paris and in Tunis, which have brought together civil society organisations that work in counter-extremism, or who engage with families, with an aim of cross-pollinating them, and incorporating them into the FATE network. At these summits, we hosted world-renowned CVE experts to share good practices and to educate our network. We ran a series of skills-building workshops at these summits, including topics such as Spotting the Signs of Radicalisation; Developing Effective Counter speech; The Role of Families in CVE; as well as collaboratively developing a FATE action plan for the two regions. Our offline events have been attended by

FATE has had active participation in 22 countries, built a consortium of 115 organisations in our network (representing 10 of the top 12 foreign terrorist fighter countries), and we have been invited back by nine network members in France, Germany, Belgium, Tunisia and Morocco to run follow-up skills-building workshops for their beneficiaries in their local areas.

We have conducted a full target audience analysis for Europe and North Africa which has shaped the counter speech we have developed centrally, campaigns that we have generated through our network members, the FATE Playbook, which we use to guide members for their work and campaigns, and the upcoming FATE online workshop modules.

Summary Metrics over first 12 months

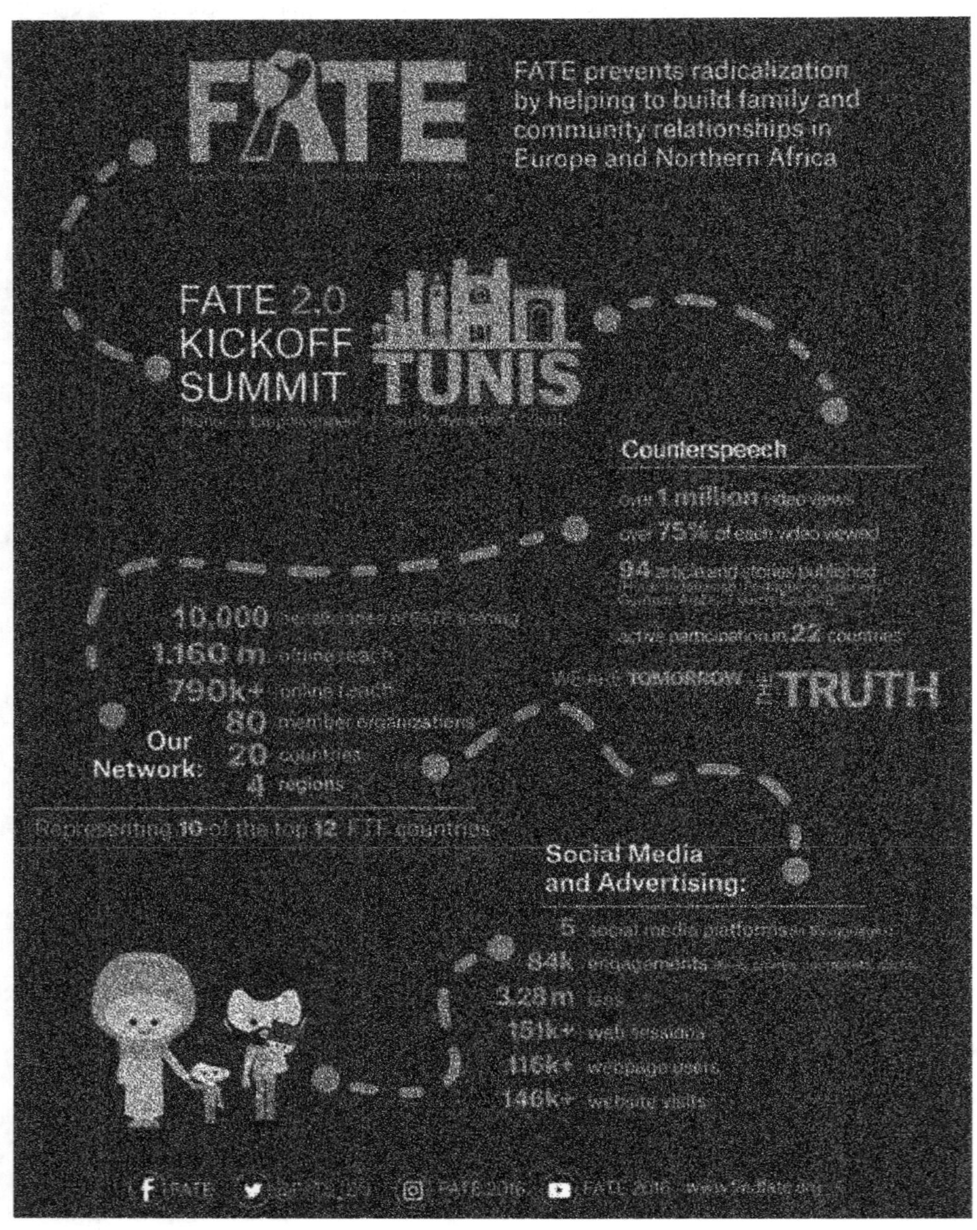

Recommendations

To challenge the persistent appeal of Islamist extremism, it is crucial that the messages its proselytisers convey are understood, publicly denounced, and meaningfully contested. Based on our analysis of the four key promises of empowerment, deliverance, participation, and piety, we put forth the following policy recommendations to address the continued appeal of Violent Extremism to women.

Our recommendations centre, reducing the exposure of individuals to Islamist propaganda and increasing resilience towards it; and furthermore, equipping families with the appropriate critical consumption skills to make this propaganda less appealing. Part of this strategy must focus on combating gender extremism, which we define as ideologies that significantly and negatively impact the human rights of one gender by control, coercion, violation, or the systemic promotion of the superiority of one gender over another

- We propose to build an even stronger network in Europe and North Africa and add a North America, Sub Saharan African and Middle Eastern network to spread the message, support network, and resources even further and build global movements. Create counter speech content and dissemination strategies for network members and offer tech solutions to them about website and apps, and creating content for campaigns

- We advocate the advanced training of women in Countering Violent Extremism (CVE) to build awareness on tackling Islamist propaganda. This should take the form of confidence training workshops for mothers, where CVE and knowledge-building on conflict situations are prioritised. Conflicts are regularly manipulated as potential grievances to be exploited by groups such as ISIS and AQ, especially if they can be used to demonstrate the idea that the West is at war with Islam.

- Teachers should also be enrolled in training modules to familiarise them with these grievances. As manifestations of institutional best practice, sessions should focus on debunking extremist claims regarding the importance and duty of marriage, the struggle against the West, and the significance of "honour".

- Relationships should be built between mothers and teachers. As such, workshops including both should be provided alongside gender extremism toolkits. All workshops, and toolkits and packages arising from them, should be delivered in multiple languages,

- Young people at risk of radicalisation often use ISIS and AQ propaganda as an authentic source of religious information. Arenas where young women can talk about spirituality beyond a religious ritualism must be encouraged. These should not be exclusively for Muslims, so they can provide spaces for active engagement and interfaith debate, enabling women to voice concerns and discuss gendered extremism.

- We recommend the utilization of media campaigns that foster female empowerment and liberation from gender violence, such as honour-based violence, female genital mutilation (FGM), and forced

- More air-time needs to be given to women who have been affected by gender extremism; they must be empowered to let other women know that they are not alone. A good example of this is the video "I Can Hold My Breath"[2] produced as a result of Quilliam' s arts, media, and outreach work. Using creative messaging, and providing a media platform for inspirational speakers, not extremists, would prevent radical groups from being able to propagandise through the mass media and claiming, as they do, to be spokespeople for the majority.

- At a community level, we advise regular workshops on life and employability skills for young women and the provision of scholarships to help women make the most of education and workforce opportunities. This will enable those at risk of radicalisation to have more, and better, opportunities. It must be encouraged and organised by governments.

- Projects that focus on empowering critical inquiry and thinking must be at the forefront of projects abroad. These will enable local communities to build resilience against narratives that may look to build on grievances and start the journey towards violent extremism

- There is a lack of consistency when it comes to programmes and projects. If programmes and projects are producing results against pre-determined criteria for success, there has to be mid and long-term determination at a Political level to ensure that programmes are continued

- The term CVE is redundant as it only focusses on combating an ideology once its manifestation becomes violent – often this is too late. We propose splitting the strategy into two parts

    - Combating Extremism – this involves empowering men and women collectively in helping to build resilience before people are radicalised
    - Terrorism Prevention – This allows for the focusing on people who may show empathy, sympathy or support for violent extremist ideas

- Working with Former Extremists and Voices that address all forms of extremism. Quilliam has over a decade of experience globally and is able to engage constructively in a meaningful way to combat extremism in all forms. Working with voices that are honest and direct, will help make the difference in making sure we are winning the fight.

---

[2] https://www.youtube.com/watch?v=UiMqbMJEYu4&feature=youtu.be

Mr. POE. Thank you very much.

Ms. Popal.

STATEMENT OF MS. FARHAT POPAL, MANAGER, WOMEN'S INITIATIVE, GEORGE W. BUSH INSTITUTE

Ms. POPAL. Chairman Poe, Representative Keating, and distinguished members of the subcommittee, it is an honor to appear here today.

My name is Farhat Popal. I work on the Women's Initiative at the non-profit nonpartisan George W. Bush Institute in Dallas, Texas. I am also Afghan American, so this issue is of great importance to me.

At the Bush Institute, we believe women are essential to the development of peaceful, open, and prosperous societies. Our Afghan Women's Project has worked to ensure the expansion of women's rights in Afghanistan and we regularly engage with remarkable leaders, from civil society advocates, to peace builders, to first ladies.

We also support Mrs. Laura Bush in her role as honorary co-chair of the U.S.-Afghan Women's Council. My comments today will focus on women's role in countering violent extremism in Afghanistan.

I will also discuss how women's meaningful inclusion in leadership can help build resilient communities. Here are the three points I would like to leave with you today.

First, Afghan women drive education, growth, and self-reliance. They are essential to Afghanistan's stability and we must continue to support them.

Second, Afghan women help build resilient communities and participate in peace building at all levels of society. We must ensure their voices are represented in the peace process.

And third, what happens elsewhere in the world matters here at home. It is in our national security and moral interest to support sustainable development in Afghanistan.

Afghan women and girls have made enormous strides in areas such as education and employment but continue to be impacted by gender-based violence, limited access to justice, and violent extremism.

In the 2017 survey of the Afghan people by the Asia Foundation, 92 percent of Afghans say they fear encountering the Taliban and 94 percent fear encountering ISIS.

I share this to show both the magnitude of the problem and the Afghan people's rejection of extremism. All Afghans benefit from effective CVE efforts but Afghan women gain the most.

They also have the most to lose if their hard-won rights are negotiated away. At the family and village level, Afghan women play a key role in mediating conflict, building trust and dialogue in the community, and counseling family members.

With over 63 percent of the population under the age of 25, mothers also can have a profound influence on their children through education.

Today, thanks to the U.S. and Afghan governments and the international community, more than 9.2 million children are enrolled in school of which almost 40 percent are girls, and the per-

centage of college-age students enrolled in higher education has
risen from 1 percent in 2001 to almost 10 percent today.

At the national level, 12 out of 63 members of the High Peace
Council are women. This visible presence is important. But women
must also have actual influence and authority.

In the 2017 initiation of the Afghan-led Kabul Process, only two
of 47 representatives were women. This marginalizes their presence and their voice.

Women have been instrumental members of provincial peace
councils, encouraging local insurgents to participate in talks and
facilitating a release of hostages.

As Chairman Poe mentioned, research shows that women's
meaningful participation in a peace negotiation makes the resulting agreement 35 percent more likely to last at least 15 years.

CVE is also about more than security. It's about creating resilient communities that are built upon strong social connections,
trust, and dialogue.

They're also built on inclusion. Afghan women are a key part of
these efforts. Last October, the Bush Institute met 14 women leaders from the Middle East, North Africa, and Afghanistan who are
advancing economic opportunity and, ultimately, peace and prosperity in their countries.

We met Nadia Behboodi of the American University of Afghanistan who is working to support women-owned businesses through
training, capital, and access to business and IT support.

We reconnected with Manizha Wafeq, featured in our book, "We
Are Afghan Women: Voices of Hope," who advocates for women's
economic rights through the Afghanistan Women Chamber of Commerce and Industry.

According to the chamber, women entrepreneurs have invested
more than $66 million in the Afghan economy and created more
than 47,000.

Afghan women have a staunch advocate in First Lady Rula
Ghani. Last fall, Ms. Ghani joined Ms. Bush on Capitol Hill in
their roles as honorary co-chairs of the U.S.-Afghan Women's Council, a key public-private partnership that was established in 2002.

They discussed the importance of advanced training and mentoring and urged us to see Afghan women as the leaders and partners they are, not as victims.

If I can leave you with one key point, it is this: Women's meaningful inclusion in all aspects of society—social, political, and economic—is essential for Afghanistan's stability and prosperity.

Here is how we can help. First, we must consider local contexts
in causes of violent extremism to inform effective CVE strategies
and women's role in them, and by building local capacity, communities can sustainably lead their own efforts.

Second, we must continue to support and fund sustainable development in Afghanistan that is aligned with national level policies
and priorities.

Stability requires equal access to justice, respect for human
rights, effective rule of law and good governance, and transparent,
effective, and accountable institutions. It also necessitates access to
quality education.

These efforts will help undermine extremist narrative and will take both public and private sector engagement.

Perhaps most importantly, we must continue to invest in women and guarantee their meaningful inclusion in peace building.

The bipartisan Women, Peace, and Security Act of 2017 is an important step in this direction but it must be implemented and funded to make a difference.

In sum, Afghan women are making a profound impact on a daily basis and it is in our interest to support them.

Thank you.

[The prepared statement of Ms. Popal follows:]

GEORGE W. BUSH INSTITUTE

Statement before the

House Committee on Foreign Affairs

Subcommittee on Terrorism, Nonproliferation, and Trade

Women's Role in Countering Terrorism

Farhat Popal

Manager, Women's Initiative, George W. Bush Institute

Tuesday, February 27, 2018

Rayburn House Office Building

Room 2172

Chairman Poe, Representative Keating, and distinguished members of the subcommittee, it is an honor to appear here today.

My name is Farhat Popal. I work on the Women's Initiative at the nonprofit, nonpartisan George W. Bush Institute in Dallas, Texas. I am also Afghan-American, born in Kabul, so this issue is near to my heart.

At the Bush Institute, we believe women are essential to the development of open, peaceful, and prosperous societies. Our initiative, the Afghan Women's Project, has worked to ensure the expansion and protection of women's rights in Afghanistan. We engage with remarkable Afghan women—educators, businesswomen, researchers, politicians, peacebuilders, and more—and support Mrs. Laura Bush in her role as Honorary Co-Chair of the U.S.-Afghan Women's Council.

My comments today will focus on women's role in countering violent extremism (CVE). I will also discuss how women's meaningful inclusion and leadership can build resilient communities.

Here are the three points I'd like to leave you with:

- Afghan women drive education, growth, and self-reliance. They are essential to Afghanistan's stability, and we must continue to invest in them.
- Afghan women help build resilient communities, and participate in peacebuilding at all levels of society. We must ensure their voices are represented in the peace process.
- What happens elsewhere in the world matters here at home. It is in our national security and moral interest to support peaceful, sustainable development in Afghanistan.

Afghan women and girls have made enormous strides in areas such as education and employment, but continue to be impacted by gender-based violence, limited access to justice, and violent extremism. Afghan girls risk acid attacks, poisoning, and kidnapping to go to school. Afghan women brave sexual harassment and violence to go to work. All Afghans endure indiscriminate bombings in their daily lives.

In the 2017 annual *Survey of the Afghan People* by The Asia Foundation, 92 percent of Afghans say they fear encountering the Taliban, and 94 percent fear encountering ISIS. I share this to show both the magnitude of the problem and the Afghan people's general lack of support for extremist groups. All Afghans benefit from effective CVE efforts and peacebuilding, but Afghan women gain the most. They also have the most to lose if their hard-won rights are negotiated away.

At the family and village level, Afghan women play a key role in mediating conflict, building trust and dialogue, educating children, and counseling family members not to engage in violence. Youth represent one of the most vulnerable groups for recruitment and radicalization. With over 63 percent of the population under the age of 25, mothers can have a profound influence on their children through education.[1] Today, thanks to the U.S. government, international community,

---

[1] "Young People," United Nations Population Fund - Afghanistan, accessed February 22, 2018, http://afghanistan.unfpa.org/node/15227.

Popal: Testimony, House Foreign Affairs Committee, Subcommittee on Terrorism, Nonproliferation, and Trade, February 27, 2018

and Afghan government efforts, more than 9.2 million children are enrolled in school, of which almost 40 percent are girls. We have seen a rise in the percentage of college-age students enrolled in higher education, from one percent in 2001 to almost 10 percent today.[2]

At the national level, 12 out of 63 members of the High Peace Council are women.[3] The visible presence of women in these bodies is important, and the Afghan government must ensure this is more than symbolic representation. Women must have actual influence and authority. In the 2017 initiation of the Afghan-led Kabul Process, only two of 47 representatives were women.[4] This marginalizes women and their voices.

At the provincial level, women have been instrumental members of provincial peace councils—encouraging local insurgents to participate in talks and facilitating the release of hostages.[5] Women's inclusion is essential to peace. Research shows women's meaningful participation in a peace negotiation makes the resulting agreement 35 percent more likely to last at least fifteen years.[6]

CVE is also about more than security. It's about creating resilient communities that are built upon strong social connections, trust, and inclusion. Afghan women are a key part of these efforts, and advancing their socioeconomic conditions, political empowerment, and voice, can foster community resilience. Many women civil society advocates are fighting for just that.

Last October, the Bush Institute hosted 14 women leaders from the Middle East, North Africa, and Afghanistan who are working to advance economic opportunity—and ultimately peace and prosperity—in their countries.

We met Nadia Behboodi, Executive Director of the International Center for Afghan Women's Economic Development at the American University of Afghanistan, where she is working to support women-owned businesses through training, capital, and access to business and information technology support.

We reconnected with Manizha Wafeq, featured in our book, *We are Afghan Women: Voices of Hope*, who advocates for women's economic rights through the Afghanistan Women Chamber of Commerce and Industry. According to the Chamber, women entrepreneurs have invested more than $66 million in the Afghan economy, and created more than 47,000 jobs.[7] When you

---

[2] "Education," USAID - Afghanistan, last updated February 21, 2018, https://www.usaid.gov/afghanistan/education.
[3] Ahmadi, Belquis. "Afghan Women Step Up in Local, National Taliban Talks," U.S. Institute of Peace, October 25, 2017, https://www.usip.org/publications/2017/10/afghan-women-step-local-national-taliban-talks.
[4] Barr, Heather. "Women Excluded Again from Afghanistan's Peace Talks," Human Rights Watch, June 6, 2017, https://www.hrw.org/news/2017/06/06/women-excluded-again-afghanistans-peace-talks.
[5] "Women's Participation in Peace Processes." Council on Foreign Relations, last updated January 5, 2018. https://www.cfr.org/interactive/womens-participation-in-peace-processes/afghanistan
[6] O'Reilly, Marie. "Why Women? Inclusive Security and Peaceful Societies," Inclusive Security, October 2015. https://www.inclusivesecurity.org/wp-content/uploads/2017/06/Why-Women-Report-2017.pdf.
[7] Afghanistan Women Chamber of Commerce and Industry, accessed February 22, 2018, http://awcci.af/en/reports/.

economically empower women, you accelerate economic recovery and advance post-conflict economies.[8]

This fall, we will launch a leadership development program focused on women who are advancing economic opportunity for all in their countries. Afghan women will be a key part of that effort.

Afghan women have a staunch advocate in First Lady Rula Ghani. Last fall, Mrs. Ghani joined Mrs. Bush on Capitol Hill in their roles as Honorary Co-Chairs of the U.S.-Afghan Women's Council. They discussed the importance of advanced training and mentoring for Afghan women, and urged us to see women as the leaders and partners they are, not as victims.

If I can leave you with one key point it is this: women's meaningful inclusion in all aspects of society—social, political, and economic—is essential for Afghanistan's stability and prosperity.

And in the words of Mrs. Bush, "As the people of Afghanistan continue on their own hard path to freedom, they must know that we are with them." Here's how we can help.

First, we must consider local contexts and causes of violent extremism to inform effective CVE strategies and women's role in them. Building local capacity enables communities to sustainably lead their own efforts.

Second, we must continue to support and fund sustainable development in Afghanistan that is aligned with national-level policies and priorities. Stability requires equal access to justice, respect for human rights, effective rule of law and good governance, and transparent, effective, and accountable institutions. It also necessitates access to quality education, particularly as insecurity and poverty threaten to undercut substantial gains in this area. These efforts will help to undermine extremist narratives, and will take both public and private sector engagement.

Perhaps most importantly, we must continue to invest in women and ensure their rights are not negotiated away in an ultimate peace agreement. We must guarantee their meaningful inclusion in peacebuilding, so they can speak for themselves. The bipartisan Women, Peace, and Security Act of 2017 is an important step in this direction, but it must be implemented and funded to make a difference.

Within their families, in their communities, and as public figures, Afghan women exhibit great leadership. They are making a profound impact on a daily basis, and it is in our interest to support them.

Thank you.

---

[8] "Preventing Conflict, Transforming Justice, Securing the Peace: A Global Study on the Implementation of the United Nations Security Council Resolution 1325," UN Women, 2015.

Mr. POE. Thank you very much.

Ms. Bigio.

STATEMENT OF MS. JAMILLE BIGIO, SENIOR FELLOW FOR WOMEN AND FOREIGN POLICY, COUNCIL ON FOREIGN RELATIONS

Ms. BIGIO. Thank you.

Chairman Poe, Ranking Member Keating, and distinguished members of the committee, thank you for the opportunity to testify before you today.

By convening this hearing, Congress is sending a bipartisan signal that the United States can no longer afford to ignore how women's participation will improve the effectiveness of counterterrorism efforts.

As you noted, extremist groups use women to their advantage, recruiting them on the one hand as facilitators and martyrs and, on the other hand, benefiting both strategically and financially from their subjugation.

A counterterrorism policy has not been as effective at understanding how women can improve security efforts. We see extremist groups target women and girls. We see some groups use sexual violence to terrorize populations, displace civilians, and generate revenue.

Extremist groups also recruit women to act as informants and facilitators. Close to 20 percent of foreign fighters from Europe who join the Islamic State are female and women have proven effective in all roles assigned to them by extremist groups including as suicide bombers.

When groups use female suicide bombers they are taking advantage of the relative absence of women in police and military forces and makes it easier for women to hide suicide devices, knowing that there is a good chance they will not encounter a female security official and therefore will not be searched.

While extremist groups are strategically using women to their advantage, there is an opportunity for counterterrorism policy to draw more on the opportunities of how women can contribute.

Women are already on the front lines of countering violent extremism, as we witness female police officers engaging with local communities to prevent violent extremism; female imams, and other religious leaders preaching religious tolerance and women countering efforts to radicalize their husbands, children, and communities.

On the military side, former U.S. Special Operations Commander Admiral William McRaven observed that including women opens up possibilities for interactions with local populations that increases the effectiveness of the overall mission.

Despite these advantages, U.S. Government policy and programs pay little attention to the role of women. To strengthen these efforts, the U.S. Government should pursue the following steps.

First, the forthcoming U.S. national counterterrorism strategy and the national strategy for countering violent extremist groups should include attention to and investment in women's roles, both in terms of how the U.S. Government can involve women leaders as well as steps to de-radicalize and reintegrate female fighters.

Efforts to address women's roles should not be detached from broader security sector policy and initiatives which result in missed opportunities where women's contributions could have improved the effectiveness of U.S. operations.

Second, to maximize the return on defense investments, the U.S. Government should increase resources to facilitate women's involvement in efforts to counterterrorism and violent extremism.

Investment by the United States in this area have been limited to small grants or standalone programs. The Defense Department, the State Department, and USAID should invest more in women's roles to counterterrorism and violent extremism.

This includes through prevention-related funds such as ESF but also security funds such as antiterrorism and law enforcement programs.

Currently, these do too little to support the role of female security officials, for example, and with the proposed cuts to diplomacy and development there's a risk that funding for women's contributions to security will be decreased, which will in turn decrease the effectiveness of U.S. security investments.

Retired General Allen, former commander of the International Security Assistance Force in Afghanistan, observed from his time that by empowering women we can make them a force to reduce the reality of radicalization, calling it an investment that pays off in virtually every occasion where I've had the opportunity to see it. He advocated increasing funding to help women counterterrorism including by making Defense Department money available for State Department-run programs in this area.

Third, the U.S. Government should address the specific needs and experiences of women. U.S. efforts to reintegrate returning fighters into communities should address the motivations and grievances of female fighters, whether in Columbia, Europe, or elsewhere.

Finally, in light of evidence that terrorists and violent extremist groups are exploiting the absence of female—of women in security sectors, U.S. security cooperation efforts should help countries to increase the recruitment, retention, and advancement of women in their security sectors.

Such efforts should target women in uniformed roles and in leadership positions in order to ensure they can shape engagements with communities and influence policy decisions.

U.S. Government training programs should require that all countries participating in U.S.-provided security and justice programs should send delegations of at least 30 percent women to ensure that women have the opportunity to benefit from our investments.

Congress and this committee can work to hold the administration accountable for ensuring that its efforts to counterterrorism and violent extremism invest in an important but overlooked strategy—the inclusion of women.

Thank you.

[The prepared statement of Ms. Bigio follows:]

COUNCIL *on*
FOREIGN
RELATIONS

February 27, 2018

Women's Contributions to Countering Terrorism and Violent Extremism

Prepared statement by
Jamille Bigio
Senior Fellow for Women and Foreign Policy
Council on Foreign Relations

Before the
House Committee on Foreign Affairs
SUBCOMMITTEE ON TERRORISM, NONPROLIFERATION, AND TRADE
United States House of Representatives
2nd Session, 115th Congress

Hearing on Women's Role in Countering Terrorism

Chairman Poe, Ranking Member Keating, distinguished members of the committee, thank you for the opportunity to testify before you today about women's roles in countering terrorism.

Extremist groups use women to their advantage—recruiting them on the one hand as facilitators and martyrs, and on the other hand benefitting both strategically and financially from their subjugation. Yet, counterterrorism policy has not been as effective at understanding how women can improve security efforts. By convening this hearing, Congress sent a bipartisan signal that the United States can no longer afford to ignore how women's participation will improve the likelihood that counterterrorism efforts are successful.

Extremist groups benefit strategically and financially from the subjugation of women
Just last week, the Nigerian militant group Boko Haram kidnapped 110 girls from their boarding school in an attack that eerily echoed the 2014 kidnapping of nearly 300 school girls from the northern city Chibok.[1] The Chibok attack spurred a local and global campaign to Bring Back Our Girls, but over 100 of those students are still being held hostage, subjected to sexual slavery and some have even been used as suicide bombers. The Chibok girls drew the world's attention, but in reality, they represent just a fraction of the thousands of women captured by the militant group during its eight-year insurgency in northern Nigeria.[2]

[1] Amanda Erickson, "Nigerians are demanding answers after another Boko Haram kidnapping," *The Washington Post*, February 25, 2017, https://www.washingtonpost.com/news/worldviews/wp/2018/02/23/nigerians-are-demanding-answers-after-another-potential-boko-haram-kidnapping/?utm_term=.4723b3e6f808.
[2] BBC News, "Nigeria's Boko Haram crisis: Dapchi anger over missing girls," *BBC News*, February 22, 2018, http://www.bbc.com/news/world-africa-43158216.

Boko Haram is not the only extremist group to target women and girls. In fact, women's rights and physical integrity are often the first targets of fundamentalists – as has been documented not only in Nigeria but also with the Taliban in Afghanistan and the self-proclaimed Islamic State in Iraq and Syria. An analysis of thirty countries across the Middle East, North Africa and South Asia found that women were substantially more likely than men to be early victims of extremism.[3]

We also know that many extremist groups benefit both strategically and financially from the subjugation of women. In recent years, conflict-related sexual violence has emerged as a core element of the ideology and operation of extremist groups, such as the Islamic State in Iraq and Syria. Both Boko Haram and the Islamic State, as well as al-Qaeda and al-Shabab, use sexual violence to terrorize populations into compliance, displace civilians from strategic areas, and entrench an ideology of suppressing women's rights to control reproduction and provide labor.[4]

Some violent extremist groups use women and girls as a form of currency in a shadow economy, generating revenue from sex trafficking, sexual slavery, and extortion through ransom. The Islamic State provides thousands of male recruits with kidnapped women and girls as wives and traps many female recruits in dorms for indoctrination and forced marriage.[5] The United Nations estimates that ransom payments extracted by the Islamic State from the Yazidi community amounted to between $35 million and $45 million in 2014 alone. And even as the Islamic State loses territory and control of physical resources, the group continues to profit from the enslavement of an estimated three thousand women and girls, many of whom are bartered and sold as commodities.[6]

This connection between gender-based violence and extremism has been found in the United States as well. According to the think tank New America's research, one-third of individuals associated with jihadist-inspired violence inside the United States had a record of domestic abuse or other sexual violence.[7]

Extremist groups recruit women to serve in a variety of roles
Extremists group don't only benefit from subjugating women; they also recruit them to act as informants, facilitators, recruiters, and martyrs. Some join voluntarily while others are forcibly recruited. Close to twenty percent of foreign fighters from Europe who joined the Islamic State are female.[8] In fact, many extremist groups have made a concerted effort to recruit women to their ranks. Some women are motivated by ideological commitment, similar to potential male fighters.[9] Others join in hopes of gaining freedoms and

---

[3] Karima Bennoune, *Your Fatwa Does Not Apply Here: Untold Stories from the Fight Against Muslim Fundamentalism* (New York: W. W. Norton & Company, 2013); Karima Bennoune, "Bennoune: Support Muslims Resisting Fundamentalism," speech delivered at the International Peace Institute, October 2, 2013, http://ipinst.org/2013/10/bennoune-support-muslims-resisting-fundamentalism; Marie O'Reilly, "Inclusive Security and Peaceful Societies: Exploring the Evidence," *Prism* 6, no. 1, March 1, 2016, pp. 21-33.
[4] Associated Press, "UN: Sexual violence increasingly used as 'terrorism' tactic," *news24*, May 16, 2017,
https://www.news24.com/World/News/un-sexual-violence-increasingly-used-as-terrorism-tactic-20170516;
[5] Erin Marie Saltman and Melanie Smith, "'Till Martyrdom Do Us Part.' Gender and the ISIS Phenomenon," Institute for Strategic Dialogue, 2015, http://www.strategicdialogue.org/wp-content/uploads/2016/02/Till_Martyrdom_Do_Us_Part_Gender_and_the_ISIS_Phenomenon.pdf.
[6] Nima Elbagir, Ghazi Balkiz, and Tamara Qiblaw, "ISIS' power is waning, but its child slave trade is still booming," *CNN*, October 18, 2017, https://www.cnn.com/2017/10/18/middleeast/isis-yazidi-slavery-child-slaves/index.html; Saudi Gazette, "Yazidi survivor won't return to Iraq for fear of new 'genocide,'" *Saudi Gazette*, February 26, 2018.
http://www.saudigazette.com.sa/article/529214/World/Mena/Yazidi-survivor-wont-return-to-Iraq-for-fear-of-new-genocide.
[7] Peter Bergen et al.,"Terrorism in America After 9/11," New America,
https://www.newamerica.org/in-depth/terrorism-in-america/.
[8] Bibi van Ginkel and Eva Entenmann, eds., "The Foreign Fighters Phenomenon in the European Union. Profiles. Threats & Policies," The International Centre for Counter-Terrorism – The Hague 7, no. 2, 2016, https://www.icct.nl/wp-content/uploads/2016/03/ICCT-Report_Foreign-Fighters-Phenomenon-in-the-EU_1-April-2016_including-AnnexesLinks.pdf.
[9] Beverley Milton-Edwards and Sumaya Attia, "Female terrorists and their role in jihadi groups," op-ed, Brookings Institution, May 9, 2017, https://www.brookings.edu/opinions/female-terrorists-and-their-role-in-jihadi-groups/.

access to resources.[10] In her recent book, Hilary Matfess observes that some Nigerian girls choose to marry into Boko Haram to receive Quranic education, in a region where only 4 percent of girls finish secondary school.[11] The Islamic State makes false promises that women will be honored as wives and mothers, exploiting a fear that Western societies do not respect Muslim women.[12] As a counterpoint, a Mercy Corps study found that the most common reason Jordanian men cited for joining the war in Syria was to protect Sunni women and children – another targeted use of women in extremist groups' radicalization efforts.[13]

And women have proven effective in all roles assigned to them by extremist groups, including as suicide bombers. In fact, in Nigeria, they have been so effective in this role—killing more than 1,200 people in the past four years—that in the last year, women have comprised close to two-thirds of the group's suicide attackers—many of whom were coerced but some whom volunteered, according to a recent report by the Combating Terrorism Center at West Point.[14]

When groups use female suicide bombers, they are taking strategic advantage of the relative absence of women in police and military forces. Female fighters can hide suicide devices under their clothing knowing that there is a good chance they will not encounter a female security official and therefore will not be searched. Extremist groups count on this limitation and the likelihood that women will move without suspicion or inspection.

As demonstrated in their attacks against women and girls, and in their recruitment and use of women as suicide bombers, extremist groups are strategically using women to their advantage. Meanwhile, the United States government is still grappling to understand the importance of women's inclusion in security efforts. It is time to catch up.

Women are on the front lines of countering extremist violence, as we witness female police officers engaging with local communities to prevent violent extremism, female imams and other religious leaders preaching religious tolerance, and women countering efforts to radicalize their husbands, children, and communities. In particular, women's inclusion in counterterrorism efforts offers three distinct advantages:

Women are well-positioned to detect early signs of radicalization, because their rights and physical integrity are often the first targets of fundamentalists. From harassment in public spaces to barriers sending their daughters to school and other challenges as communities become more segregated—women are substantially more likely than men to be early victims of extremism.[15]

Women's central roles in many families and communities also afford them a unique vantage point from which to recognize unusual patterns of behavior and signs of impending conflict. In Afghanistan, for example,

---

[10] International Crisis Group, "Nigeria: Women and the Boko Haram Insurgency," Report 242, December 2016, https://www.crisisgroup.org/africa/west-africa/nigeria/nigeria-women-and-boko-haram-insurgency.
[11] The Economist, "More than meets the eye: Women and Boko Haram," book review, *The Economist*, November 13, 2017, https://www.economist.com/news/books-and-arts/21731805-outrages-islamist-group-obscure-ineptitude-nigerian-state-rotten.
[12] Erin Marie Saltman and Melanie Smith, "'Till Martyrdom Do Us Part.' Gender and the ISIS Phenomenon."
[13] MercyCorps. "From Jordan to jihad: the lure of Syria's violent extremism groups." MercyCorps, Policy Brief, 2015, https://www.mercycorps.org/sites/default/files/From%20Jordan%20to%20Jihad_0.pdf.
[14] Conor Gaffey, "ISIS just started using female suicide bombers, but Boko Haram has been doing it for years—and shows no sign of stopping," *Newsweek*, August 12, 2017, http://www.newsweek.com/isis-boko-haram-nigeria-suicide-bomber-649790; Vladimir Hernandez & Stephanie Hegarty. "Made-up to look beautiful. Sent out to die. The young women sent into crowds to blow themselves up," *BBC News*, 2018, http://www.bbc.co.uk/news/resources/idt-sh/made_up_to_look_beautiful_sent_out_to_die; Jason Warner and Hilary Matfess, "Exploding Stereotypes: The Unexpected Operational and Demographic Characteristics of Boko Haram's Suicide Bombers," Combating Terrorism Center at West Point, United States Military Academy, August 2017, https://ctc.usma.edu/app/uploads/2017/08/Exploding-Stereotypes-1.pdf.
[15] Karima Bennoune, *Your Fatwa Does Not Apply Here: Untold Stories from the Fight Against Muslim Fundamentalism*; Karima Bennoune, "Bennoune: Support Muslims Resisting Fundamentalism." Marie O'Reilly, "Inclusive Security and Peaceful Societies: Exploring the Evidence."

women reported that young men were being recruited at weddings. Their concerns went unheeded, and the young men they had observed went on to kill 32 civilians on a bus.[16] In Libya too, women warned of rising radicalism: Analysts observed a flow of Western female recruits, consistent with a need for wives as the Islamic State established a headquarters there.[17] At the same time, local women reported increasing infringements on their rights, including being harassed for driving alone.[18] And again, these warning went unheeded, providing the Islamic State additional time to establish itself before counterterrorism efforts ramped up.

Women are well-positioned to mitigate radicalization. Recent research shows that anti-terrorism messages are disseminated quite effectively throughout families and communities by women, who can challenge extremist narratives in homes, schools and social environments. They have particular influence among youth populations, and are strategically placed to serve as a buffer between radical influences and those who are next to be targeted.

Despite this, traditional efforts by governments and nongovernmental organizations to combat radicalization rarely include women—they typically focus on reaching out to political or religious leaders, who are predominantly male. Slowly, countries are learning. Morocco, for example, recognizing women's influence in their families and communities, educates women to become religious scholars and sends them out to where radical Islamists target disenfranchised youth for recruitment.[19]

As security officials, women provide distinct insights and information that can be mission-critical in keeping the peace. Female security officials help ensure that female fighters cannot move freely by conducting searches in culturally appropriate ways. They may have access to populations and sites that men do not, allowing them to gather critical intelligence about potential security threats.[20] Furthermore, women's participation in the military and police has been shown to improve how a local community perceives law enforcement—which, in turn, improves the ability to provide security.[21]

Former U.S. Special Operations Command Commander Admiral William McRaven observed that "including women allows tailored, culturally sensitive engagement, opening up possibilities for interactions with local populations that would otherwise be closed to all-male teams. These contributions increase the effectiveness of the overall mission as women positively shape the wartime environment and, in some instances, prevent conflict from occurring in the first place."[22]

---

[16] Wazhma Frogh, "Imagine If the Minister Had Listened to Us," speech delivered at Inclusive Security, October 15, 2015, https://www.inclusivesecurity.org/2016/04/14/imagine-minister-listened-us/.

[17] Anne-Marie Slaughter and Elizabeth Weingarten, "A national security blind spot," *The Straits Times*, October 28, 2016, http://www.straitstimes.com/opinion/a-national-security-blind-spot.

[18] Swanee Hunt, Esther Ibanga, and Alaa Murabit, "On GPS: Women waging peace," video interview at CNN, January 4, 2016, http://www.cnn.com/videos/tv/2016/01/04/exp-gps-0103-hunt-ibanga-murabit.cnn.

[19] Dina Temple-Raston. "The Female Quran Experts Fighting Radical Islam in Morocco: 'The women scholars here are even more important than men," *The Atlantic*, February 12, 2018, https://www.theatlantic.com/international/archive/2018/02/the-female-quran-experts-fighting-radical-islam-in-morocco/551996/?utm_source=twb.

[20] Louise Olsson and Johan Tejpar, eds., *Operational Effectiveness and UN Resolution 1325 – Practices and Lessons from Afghanistan*, (FOI, 2009), pg. 117; pp. 126-127; Tobie Whitman and Jacqueline O'Neill, "Attention to gender increases security in operations: Examples from the North Atlantic Treaty Organization (NATO)," The Institute for Inclusive Security, April 2012, pp. 7-13.

[21] Kim Lonsway et al.; "Policy Briefing Paper: Gender Sensitive Police Reform in Post Conflict Societies," United Nations Development Fund for Women and United Nations Development Program, October 2007, http://unwomen.org/~/media/Headquarters/Media/Publications/UNIFEM/GenderSensitivePoliceReformPolicyBrief2007eng.pdf; Tara Denham, "Police Reform and Gender," Geneva Center for the Democratic Control of Armed Forces (DCAF), 2008, p. 5.

[22] William H. McRaven, "Women in Special Operations Forces: Advancing Peace and Security through Broader Cultural Knowledge," in *Women on the frontlines of peace and security*, (NDU Press, 2014). pg. 127.

Despite the evidence of women's contributions to preventing and mitigating violent extremism, U.S. government policy and programs pay little attention to the role of women. Some critics will suggest that expending money and time to advance women's roles in countering violent extremism would be an unnecessary distraction. This is false, misleading, and ultimately dangerous. Engaging women from the outset is necessary for long-term success. The Women, Peace, and Security Act of 2017 requires the U.S. government to increase women's participation in peace and security efforts—and that includes in efforts to counterterrorism. I've outlined here a few suggestions based on the gaps I observed while serving on the National Security Council staff and at the U.S. departments of state and of defense.

To strengthen counterterrorism efforts, the U.S. government should pursue the following steps:

First, the forthcoming U.S. national strategy for countering violent extremist groups should include attention to and investment in women's roles. As the evidence shows, women are influential in whatever capacity they serve—whether as moderating and peaceful forces in a community or as extremist fighters. The new countering violent extremism strategy—required by the 2018 National Defense Authorization Act—should outline how the U.S. government will involve women leaders and women's groups, as well as identify necessary steps to deradicalize and reintegrate female fighters. Current State Department and USAID efforts to lay out a policy on including women in countering violent extremism should not remain isolated from the forthcoming broader strategy. This has been the challenge to date: Most efforts to address these issues have remained detached from broader security-sector policy and initiatives, resulting in many missed opportunities where women's contributions could have improved the effectiveness of U.S. operations. Shifting this trend requires a new level of commitment by the United States and holds the potential to significantly improve efforts to counter terrorism and violent extremism around the world.

Second, to maximize the return on defense investments, the U.S. government should increase resources to facilitate women's involvement in efforts to counter terrorism and violent extremism. Investment by the United States in this area has been limited to small grants or stand-alone programs. The United States also has not leveraged its leadership position to encourage other governments to make security-sector commitments on this issue. DOD, the State Department, and USAID should invest in women's roles to counter terrorism and violent extremism. This includes through prevention-related funds, but also security funds, such as antiterrorism and law enforcement programs. With the significant cuts to diplomacy and development efforts proposed in the current budget process, there is a risk that funding for women's contributions to security will be decreased, which will in turn decrease the effectiveness of U.S. security investments.

It is also important to make it easier for proponents of women's involvement in deradicalization efforts to access funding—whether in militaries, police, government, or civil society. Retired General John Allen, former commander of the International Security Assistance Force in Afghanistan and former special presidential envoy to the global coalition to counter the self-proclaimed Islamic State, has advocated increasing funding to help women fight radicalization, including by making Defense Department money available for State Department–run programs. As Allen reflected, by "empowering [women], we can make them a force to reduce the reality of radicalization," calling it an "investment [that] pays off in virtually every occasion where I've had the opportunity to see it."[23]

Third, the U.S. government should address the specific needs and experiences of women, whether as victims, mitigators, or perpetrators. U.S. efforts to reintegrate returning fighters into communities should address their motivations and grievances—whether in Colombia, Europe, or elsewhere. United States support for political, religious, and security leaders should prioritize female leaders, who are well-placed to challenge extremist narratives. The United States should encourage governments to classify survivors of sexual

---

[23] John Allen, "Countering Violent Extremism by Engaging Women," roundtable event at the Council on Foreign Relations, December 7, 2016, https://www.cfr.org/event/countering-violent-extremism-engaging-women.

violence by terrorist or extremist groups as victims of terrorism, and thereby ensure a greater level of support. Extremist groups employ sexual violence as a tool to denigrate the enemy, create stigma, and unravel protective kinship networks. Counterterrorism efforts should undermine these efforts to isolate victims and weaken communities.

Finally, in light of evidence that terrorist and violent extremist groups are including women and exploiting their absence in security sectors, U.S. security cooperation efforts should provide technical assistance to increase the recruitment, retention, and advancement of women in security sectors. Such efforts should target women in uniformed roles and in leadership positions, in order to ensure they can both shape engagement with communities and influence policy decisions with their unique perspectives on communities' experiences. Effective measures to promote women's participation in security roles include quotas, fast-track promotion plans, legal prohibitions on discrimination against women, and support for networking and professional development. In addition, the U.S. government should require all countries participating in U.S.-provided security and justice programs—from the International Military Education and Training program to courses offered at the Department of Defense's regional centers—to send delegations that are at least 30 percent female, a threshold that research suggests affords a critical mass to enable women's influence.[24]

Both to strengthen the U.S. military and to lead by example, the United States should take steps to increase the proportion of women in the U.S. military and across law enforcement by doubling recruitment, promotion, and retention efforts and maintaining rigorous implementation of antidiscrimination laws.

Congress and this Committee can work to hold the administration accountable for ensuring that its efforts to counter terrorism and violent extremism invest in an important but overlooked strategy: the inclusion of women. Preventing and countering violent extremism and terrorism in the 21st century requires unleashing the potential of 50 percent of the world's population. It is not just the right thing to do—it is a strategic imperative to advance national security.

Thank you, Mr. Chairman, for this opportunity to testify.

---

[24] Rosabeth Moss Kanter, *Men and Women of the Corporation* (New York: Basic Books, 1997), pp. 381–395.

6

Mr. POE. Thank you very much. I will now recognize myself for questions.

I appreciate your very good information about an issue that has not gotten much attention at all on the fight against terrorism since 9/11 and really before that, and so I want to speak on behalf of all—the entire subcommittee that we appreciate your testimony and also your written testimony as well. It is fascinating.

Let me ask this question to all four of you. You have given us a lot of information—good information, valuable information.

I hope that in the fight against terrorism, if we can use that word, we refocus on the importance of the role of women in solving this problem but also in seeing how intricately entwined women are in the whole process of fighting terrorism—women as victims, women as enablers, women as problem solvers—all three.

So be specific in what we can do right now to change this focus and include the role of women in those areas I mentioned, primarily in fighting extremism and being enablers of extremism, if I can use those two concepts.

If you can just be specific—I will start with you, Dr. Hudson.

Ms. HUDSON. Thank you, Chairman Poe. Very nice to address that very important question.

In my line of work at the Bush School, we look at intel quite a bit and one of the things that I've argued in previous publications is that we are not tracking the types of things that we need to track.

We could have been much more aware of what was going on with groups such as Boko Haram if we had been tracking things such as bride price trajectories.

One of the most fascinating pieces of research I saw came from the West African situation, which has been roiled by civil war, and they found that the rebel groups were—had so much more success recruiting in areas where the rate of polygamy had risen as a result of economic setbacks, pricing young men out of the market.

There's also, I think, early warning to be seen in things such as sex ratio alterations. You know, we think of there being a deficit of girls in China and India.

But do you know there's now 19 nations that have abnormal birth sex ratios? And they include nations that definitely need to be on our radar screen—Azerbaijan, Armenia, Moldova, Albania, and others.

What I am suggesting is that the means by which women are subordinated in these types of societies through bride price, through polygamy, through sex ratio alteration has to be part of our intelligence gathering—has to be part of our situational awareness and of our understanding of early warning indicators.

We've not seen that to date and that is certainly something that I would work on. And I will yield the floor, but I will also say that disrupting women's disempowerment at the household level, focussing on things like property rights, inheritance rights, focussing on things such as child custody, divorce, age at marriage, this is where the rubber hits the road for the empowerment of women.

We have found that it's absolutely possible to disempower women and yet have a high female literacy rate, a high female labor force participation rate, high female representation in Parliament.

Those things don't touch the lives of women at the household level where their voice will either be heard or ignored. So disrupting that syndrome is also important.

Mr. POE. Mr. Rafiq.

Mr. RAFIQ. Thank you, Chairman Poe, for your question.

I think it's a very good question and I think that there is a broader answer and then a more specific answer.

The broader answer is that too often governments at the U.S. and the U.K.—my home country—we suffer from a lack of political consistency and the will to see things through.

Even over the last 10 years, there have been a number of very, very good projects which have established criterias of success and the metrics have been achieved and then after a year it has been decided that those projects aren't going to be carried on or supported anymore.

But to be more specific, you asked for one or two clear things. I think, first of all, you know, people talk about this being a problem of Islam and then other people say it's got nothing to do with Islam.

The reality is it's somewhere in the middle. It has something to do with certain interpretations of Islam. And one of the things that we need to do within certainly Western countries a lot more is help women become at the forefront of reform.

Theological reform is absolutely critical to solving this problem and it's reform around gender extremism but also a reform around what the role of women can be within Muslim communities.

But too many people, too many families, too many Muslims that live in either the U.K. or the U.S. are living almost parallel lives. There is the rule of law and what's expected and what—of women generally and what is allowed—what women are allowed to do generally and then there are women within certainly more conservative fundamentalist families and households. I think that reform is absolutely critical. But women need to be at the forefront of that.

The other thing I think that's very, very important is if we look at the deliverance, the piety, the empowerment promises that groups like ISIS have, we have to take that away from them and we have to encourage Muslim women who are in the U.S. and around the world to become—take leadership roles in actually—taking on more mainstream civil society projects because if we can do that, that'll take away the lure from groups like al-Qaeda and ISIS, and I think that this is something that can be done both in the offline world and in the online world.

You know, people talk about the internet radicalizing people. Well, nobody goes online to buy a pair of shoes or a handbag and somebody ends up becoming a jihadist or a jihadi bride.

They need to be looking for something and far too—there are far too many messages online that are actually recruiting young female people—young women and we need to help young women flood the internet with good ideas.

Mr. POE. Thank you. I am out of time, so if we have time we'll come back to the last two witnesses to answer that question. So save your answers that you wrote notes about.

I yield to the gentleman from Massachusetts, the ranking member, Mr. Keating.

Mr. KEATING. Thank you, Mr. Chairman.

Ms. Bigio, I was—I recall a period when I think the earliest or among the earlier training of women police, I was in Afghanistan. General Allen was there at the time, as you mentioned. I got to see some of the early training and actually participate a little bit from my former law enforcement role before I got to Congress.

But I am curious, since then are there more women training women now? I mean, back then, it was multi-country training but it was men getting involved in a lot of that training.

Are women training women? Have you seen that and how successful has that been? I often envision some of our own U.S. police officers going over there, training as well. But can you comment on that?

Ms. BIGIO. Thank you for the important question. And as you note, there have been some programs which the U.S. Government has invested in training women in security sectors and the police and military and working to help increase their representation.

There's far too little being done right now by the U.S. Government in our—in the U.S. Government security cooperation programs to really help ensure that women have the opportunity serve and to contribute whether in uniform or in policy making roles.

Mr. KEATING. Yes, I do believe that. I believe that it's one thing to train. It's another thing to show the example——

Ms. BIGIO. Right.

Mr. KEATING [continuing]. That there are women doing that in our country as well. So thank you.

Another important question I had for all of you, if you will, because it's one that I find very difficult for us as a barrier. Let me use the example of early-age marriage, which I am sure Dr. Hudson has done research in, too, in the school.

How do we deal with the cultural norms? It's great that we are coming in and we want to do some of these things. We are beginning to get statistics and recognize the problems before they really incubate to a greater extent.

Now, how do we deal with that? I mean, these countries, for instance, with early-age marriages that's the norm or it's culturally accepted there.

What kind of barriers are there and how can we overcome some of those barriers?

Ms. HUDSON. That's terrific. Actually, that's one of the core issues, I think, that breeds unstable societies. I want to make a general comment and then make some specific comments and then defer to my colleagues.

I know the CFR has done some terrific work on child marriage. I want to make sure that Ms. Bigio also can answer here.

But the first one is the notion that it's cultural is very interesting because we've seen striking success in regionally-based pacts, if you will—mutual understanding—to raise the marriage age.

So in societies where we've seen very low age of marriage, by law the marriage age is now being raised. Okay.

Now, of course, as you can imagine, there's a huge disconnect between the new law and what's actually happening on the ground. But the first step was getting the law changed and we've seen stunning success in that over the past 10 years.

The second thing that has to do—that you have to do once you have the law changed is to change the incentive structure.

In bride price societies, fathers of the bride can't marry off their sons until they've married off their daughters first to get the bride price so they can then afford to pay the bride price back to their sons' wives' family and that pushes the age of marriage down for girls vis-a-vis the age of marriage for boys.

And so we can begin to disrupt these bride price societies and we've seen some fascinating programs that attempt to offset the incentive to, in a sense, sell off these girls young.

So I think on a conceptual level, change is possible. We've seen it in the raising of the age of marriage for girls across continents and, second of all, we've seen some very innovative programming which the U.S. could back that begins to disrupt these types of syndromes.

Ms. BIGIO. I would note, just an addition on innovative programs is—are opportunities to invest more in education so where we see incentives for girls to continue their education through secondary schools that that helps to raise the age in which they marry.

Mr. KEATING. Great.

Just quickly, I just offer you all the opportunity—if you have—you think there are portals where we can get involved directly in an oversight capacity or there are upcoming opportunities to comment on issues that could be important as well as learn more about some of the things that are working, if you could feel free to contact us in the future as we move forward on this. If we can be helpful intervening or at least advocating for these things.

And I will yield back, Chairman. I have a lot of other questions. This is really an important hearing we are having.

Mr. POE. I thank the gentleman.

The chair will recognize the gentleman from Virginia, Mr. Garrett.

Mr. GARRETT. Thank you, Mr. Chairman. I thank the witnesses for being here.

I am going to take this opportunity to pound a drum that the members of the committee who are here have heard me pound before and perhaps you haven't and I hope you will join me and assist me.

While I sit on this side of the chair, which might indicate a party affiliation, I was not elected by my constituents to serve along the lines or ideas of any particular individual whether they occupy this August legislative body or a beautiful white home on 1600 Pennsylvania Avenue, and I am a staunch advocate of the McGovern-Dole school feeding program which we have seen cuts in over the past year—not only cuts but proposed further cuts.

I would speak to essentially the reduction and radicalization amongst males in a populace wherein females are empowered by virtue of education.

I would ask you all if that's not an accurate characteristic, and I am going to bounce around the committee with no intended offense.

Ms. Bigio, am I pronouncing it right? Where you see more educated women do you see a reduction in radicalization amongst the male population? And I got—and I apologize because I am running on a timer.

And so what the school feeding program does is creates an alternative to a paradigm where in a world of subsistence farming a mother and father might need to choose whether to put their daughter in a field to essentially cultivate the food that she might eat or where they might allow her to gain an education because the food that she needs in order to live is provided in exchange, essentially, for that education. Is that an accurate characterization, Mr. Rafiq?

Mr. RAFIQ. Yes, absolutely.

Mr. GARRETT. Again, and I apologize for how I do this. But I hope that there are people listening not only in this room but across this country and this city and across the world.

And so when you see female educational attainment we also see a corresponding rise in economic opportunity within a society for both men and women. Is that generally accurate, Ms. Popal?

Ms. POPAL. Yes, it is.

Mr. GARRETT. And so when you see that rise in economic empowerment we see a corresponding rise in things like hope and it's perhaps cliche but probably quite real that a young person who has hope to aspire toward some dream or goal in the future is less likely to strap a bomb vest to themselves, for example. Is that broadly accurate, Ms. Hudson?

Ms. HUDSON. Absolutely. Grievance comes from despair.

Mr. GARRETT. And so the problem that I would see with this program is that it's hard to quantify the terrorists who were never created. In other words, we invest on the front end.

We don't know what horrible acts we've prevented on the back end and then a way that we can do this that empowers not just women but people is school feeding programs which encourages the education of young women, which elevates almost uniformly entire societies and leads to a reduction in radicalization.

I've got 2 minutes remaining. If you all can try to keep to 30 seconds.

Dr. Hudson, would you—and just bounce down the line—speak to what you think might be positive outcomes of school feeding and if this might help empower women and reduce radicalization in nations where these sorts of things are a problem.

Ms. HUDSON. Absolutely. The education of young people, both female and male, offers greater opportunities for economic advancement for them personally and for their families.

It also offers them larger horizons in terms of greater knowledge about their world and their place in it and what they can do for good.

So in all measures, both for girls and for boys, keeping them in school and allowing them a basic education through school feeding programs is laudatory.

Mr. GARRETT. Thank you. And I think it was—I believe, and I might misquote here—General Mattis, who said, "We can either provide foreign aid or we can start buying more bombs and bullets."

And having served in the military, I understand that there's a time and a place for everything. But I would rather help people than kill them.

Mr. Rafiq, if you could speak to school feeding and the potential to help women and thus help reduce radicalization and reduce terrorism.

Mr. RAFIQ. I think, certainly, it's one of the strategies that will pay off some dividends. However, I think there is a mistake to think that lack of education is the thing that actually drives extremism and terrorism.

The World Bank did a survey of foreign fighters in ISIS joint territory—held territory and they found that the overwhelming majority of people had a higher education, a higher social standing than the national average of the countries that they came from.

Zawahiri, the current leader of al-Qaeda, is a leading surgeon—doctor. Bin Laden was an engineer, and there are many, many other people.

Mr. GARRETT. And we certainly saw this, right, and I think the bin Laden is an engineer paradigm is a great one. But we saw this even during the mujahedeen's fight against the Soviet Union in Afghanistan.

Having said that, it was almost a rite of passage and I would point out that the countries from which these fighters generally come are countries where women aren't empowered economically and oftentimes aren't educated. So it might be a chicken-and-egg scenario.

I apologize. I am out of time. May I—would the chair indulge me for 45 seconds so I can let Ms. Popal and Ms. Bigio have a moment?

Mr. POE. I will indulge you, but you can get more questions asked in 5 minutes than anybody I've ever met. So—and fast as well. But yes, you may.

Mr. GARRETT. I just love being able to lead, Judge.

Ms. Popal, if you could speak to it.

Ms. POPAL. Yes. I actually would like to share just an example. One of the women in our book, "We Are Afghan Women: Voices of Hope," Razia Jan, is the founder of the Zabuli Education Center.

It's a private K through 12 girls' school that provides more than 500 girls in Afghanistan with free education, uniforms, shoes, warm coats, and meals.

That school has changed men's attitudes so much so that they're willing to protect it and to send their daughters to college, and this is just one concrete example that I wanted to share with you all.

Mr. GARRETT. Thank you.

Ms. Bigio—apologize if I get it wrong.

Ms. BIGIO. Thank you.

No, it's critical that you're focussing on this—on this important issue. We certainly see that providing opportunities for women and girls including for education is what seeds the ground for them to be able to contribute fully to their society.

And when you have space in the education programs where you have boys and girls learning together, engaging in dialogue together, it forms an avenue for them to look at solving problems together in their societies as well.

And so you're bringing all of your resources in that country together to advance and pursue opportunities that will then help to counter radicalization efforts.

I thank you all. Thanks to the chair and the other members for their indulgence.

Mr. POE. I thank the gentleman from Virginia.

The chair recognizes the gentle lady from Florida, Ms. Frankel, who was the person who had the idea to have this hearing. I will recognize the gentle lady from Florida.

Ms. FRANKEL. Thank you. It takes a woman, right?

Mr. POE. That's right.

Ms. FRANKEL. So thank you, Mr. Poe. Thank you, gentlemen, for having this hearing. Thank you, witnesses.

I am very taken by Dr. Hudson—your testimony that there were 11 indicators of empowerment at the household level that you say are the strongest predictor of terrorism.

Could you quickly tell me what they are?

Ms. HUDSON. I brought all of my printouts for you if you ever wanted to see them. [Laughter.]

Ms. FRANKEL. Oh, I would like to see them.

Ms. HUDSON. Our 11 measures——

Mr. POE. Without objection, they will be made part of the record.

Ms. HUDSON. Oh, okay.

Ms. FRANKEL. That would be terrific. Okay. That would be great.

Ms. HUDSON. May I just preface it by telling you an anecdote, which is that about 10 years ago I had a critical conversation with an Afghan female member of Parliament and I was gushing naively about how empowered she was and, you know, new generation of Afghan women.

And she said, "Valerie, I could go home today and my husband could say, 'I divorce you' three times and I would be divorced, and I would have nothing from my household. I would not be able to take anything with me. I would not have any place to go."

She said, "Even if I don't get divorced, I may have no say in when my daughters and sons marry and who they marry, right. How empowered am I really?" And I realized that my focus on these broader measures was beside the point.

We really need to look at the straitjacket under which women live within their own households, according to marriage and personal status law.

So we look at things such as patrilocal marriage—does the bride have to move to the groom's household upon marriage—polygymy, cousin marriage, bride price, level of domestic violence within the home, whether there's female sanction for femicide in the home and whether you can have legal exemption if you rape a woman if you offer to marry her. So——

Ms. FRANKEL. Let me just—let me ask you this. How did you come up with the 11 indicators or did you first look at factors that correlate with terrorism or you knew what the 11 were?

Ms. HUDSON. No. What we had done is based on almost 20 years of research. We understood that cage that's right there at the household level and it's a cage that is created through marriage law and personal status law and property rights that disempowers the woman specifically within her household.

So she can't access the resources. She doesn't have the say within her household. She can be beaten in her household, and so forth.

Ms. FRANKEL. So just to get the correlation with the—with the terrorism, is this making women less effective in terms of stopping——

Ms. HUDSON. You bet.

Ms. FRANKEL [continuing]. Their son or maybe even their daughter from becoming—okay.

Ms. HUDSON. Absolutely right.

Ms. FRANKEL. What I am curious—I mean, I don't want to start a fight here—is what the other three of you think of this research.

Mr. RAFIQ. I think the research is absolutely fantastic and I agree on the whole. But I think we have to recognize something— that women from Western countries have left societies where they have had—they've had full rights or perceived to have full rights within the law and they've decided to go and join ISIS for even less rights.

They've decided to go and join ISIS where they could be beaten up. They could—they could have—their husbands could have more than one wife and, in many cases, did, and they decide to go there.

So I think just to look at the grievances on their own I think is not enough because——

Ms. FRANKEL. But she—I think she's talking—are you talking about, though, the grievances where the terrorism is actually taking place or——

Ms. HUDSON. When I talk about grievances, I am focussing on the grievances that young men experience that make them prey to these recruiters.

So grievances over bride price, grievances over scarcity of women, grievances over lack of economic opportunity.

So I completely agree with Dr. Rafiq that one of the most interesting things is to examine the situation of young women who have left countries that supposedly guarantee their rights to join places like ISIS that don't. But actually I don't think we disagree.

Ms. FRANKEL. No, I think—because I—okay, because I'm just trying to understand this. I think you're talking about factors that are actually motivating the men to become terrorists——

Ms. HUDSON. Yes. Right.

Ms. FRANKEL [continuing]. Because the women are being segregated and there's not enough women to marry. I am just saying, there's not enough women to marry or there's not enough mothers to say, don't do this kind of thing.

I would like to hear the other two—what you think.

Ms. POPAL. So I think in the context of Afghanistan, you have a lot of women in rural areas who don't have the same opportunities that women in urban areas have and generally the level of education and the level of literacy is lower.

But I think it's important to remember that, you know, sustainable development programs, if done correctly, can really have an impact on the household level. So it doesn't necessarily have to start in the household and move outward. It can start outward and move inward.

One example is the National Solidarity program. It's a government development program that created democratically-elected community development councils and women have been a part of these councils in Afghanistan that essentially fund small-scale development projects.

And one evaluation showed that the National Solidarity program increases girls' school attendance, their quality of learning.

It increases child doctor and prenatal visits, the probability that a woman would be able to go see a doctor for her illness.

It even creates sort of a durable increase in the provision of local government services specifically for women and it increases men's acceptance of female political participation and their participation in local governance.

So I think that's important to remember.

Ms. BIGIO. I agree with—that it's critical that we look at what are the barriers that are preventing women from fully participating in society and some of these are legal.

They're also cultural and structural barriers that prevent women from engaging in contributing in their families, in their communities, in government, in decision making roles in the security sector.

And as we discussed earlier, it's critical that those policies and programs are shaped by the insights and perspectives that women can bring and their engagement with communities.

So if there are laws or other barriers that are preventing women from engaging fully, then the resulting policies and programs will not be as effective in making sure—in promoting security in their countries.

So it is critical to look at the legal, structural, and cultural barriers in a country that are preventing women from being full participants and in promoting security.

Ms. FRANKEL. Thank you. My time is up. But I hope—maybe, Mr. Poe, when you—your turn is up, I know—when they get back to you—you had asked them to all give their suggestions.

What we haven't heard, which I hope they can relay, is what is our State Department—what do our Federal agencies need to start doing better. That would be of good help to us.

Mr. POE. The chair recognizes the gentleman from Illinois, Mr. Schneider.

Mr. SCHNEIDER. Thank you, and I want to thank the chair and the ranking member for having this meeting, my colleague from Florida for suggesting this meeting, and especially to the witnesses for your testimony today.

This has been eye opening. I think we are talking about a very important issue.

I am going to start with Ms. Bigio. You sparked a thought and it actually may relate to what Ms. Frankel was saying on policy making.

You used the sense of we want to have at least 30 percent of the people on the ground as women. I think as we go into these programs, whether it is in uniform or not in uniform, should the programs—I am going to frame this—feel free to push back on it—is it better that we are doing separate programs for women?

Parallel programs for women that we might be doing at the same time for men, integrated programs where it is for both women and men and putting that foot forward—does that make any sense?

Ms. BIGIO. It does, and I thank you for that great question.

So there is incredible value in integrated programming and ensuring that men and women are together, learning and setting a norm that it is through the participation of men and women together in society serving side by side in the military, in the police, in legislatures, in government that together, combining their insights and perspectives, they will put forward the strongest and most effective policies and programs and strategies.

So it is critical that we invest and continue to pursue programs like that, which is why the 30 percent quota is making sure that there are women represented there.

Now, there is an importance of targeted programming to provide women with professional development, networking, mentoring, to help them fast track their careers in sectors where they have been under represented.

So when you're looking at programs to help increase representation of women in the police and military, for example, it's important to have training programs where they are working side by side with the male colleagues with whom they will serve, and it's also important to create networking and professional development opportunities for them so that they can discuss and address the barriers that they are sharing and experiencing in their careers.

Mr. SCHNEIDER. All right. And this maybe is for the entire panel— I would imagine then in many of these communities having integrated programs is going to face resistance—that people will push back.

How can we work with our resources with communities in which we are engaged to address that push back and create a resiliency to overcome those who are against us?

Ms. BIGIO. So yes, wherever these programs are offered they should be done in a culturally appropriate way.

So first off, when people come to participate in training programs here in the U.S. Government, in regional center—in the Defense Department's regional security studies programs, for example, or in other programs here, that's an opportunity where men and women are training together and are learning together.

So in the programs that we offer that's a critical space to ensure that we set aside slots and make sure that women have the opportunity to participate where right now they do not.

In countries where there are different cultural practices, there it's taking the lead from our partners in the governments to understand what's the structure and set-up that will both—that will best fit with the overall goal recognizing men and women are serving together then in those sectors in Afghanistan and Iraq.

Men and women are serving together in the police, and so we do want to ensure that there are training programs and other areas where they are practicing that.

Mr. SCHNEIDER. Anyone else want to add to that?

Well, thank you. With that—Mr. Rafiq?

Mr. RAFIQ. No, I was just going to say that I think sometimes we have to be pragmatic and recognize that in some countries, for example, let's pick Saudi Arabia.

If we were wanting to run programs in Saudi Arabia, it's just not going to be possible to be able to currently have programs where men and women are actually being trained together, and sometimes we have to take low-hanging fruit and eventually work to a situation where we can get and empower those countries to be in situations where they can have men and women working together and training together.

Mr. SCHNEIDER. Thank you.

With that, I yield back.

Mr. POE. I thank the gentleman.

I am going to ask the last two witnesses the question that I asked the first two witnesses, and I am sure you remember the question.

The question was, what can we do right now about this issue? Ms. Popal? And I want to thank you—I want to thank all of you. But I am fascinated with your background and you have tremendous insight into this very specific issue, as all four of you do.

But go ahead.

Ms. POPAL. Thank you.

I wanted to talk about two——

Mr. POE. Microphone on?

Ms. POPAL. Oh. I wanted to talk about two issues, just briefly.

The first one is just reiterating the—reiterating the importance of education and really building critical thinking skills in women to be able to challenge some of these extremist narratives and allow them the confidence and the voice to be able to speak up and do that.

There have been studies out there that have interviewed women and, unfortunately, there is not a lot of robust data on the role of women and countering violent extremism in Afghanistan.

But what does exist really points to the fact that women do get listened to within the household but a lot of times they don't have the confidence, or they don't have the knowledge, or they don't have the education or the literacy to be able to push back in a way that make sense. So that would be one thing.

The other point I wanted to talk about is just the importance of advancing economic opportunity. We, at the Bush Institute, are working on promoting a women's leadership program that focuses on women who are advancing economic opportunity for everyone, not just for other women, in their communities and their countries. And this is a multi-country program. It spans the Middle East, North Africa, and Afghanistan, and it's an effort to really show the value that women bring to societies as a whole.

So, again, education and economic opportunity are two ways that we can work toward sustainable development in Afghanistan and that in and of itself will help counter violent extremism.

Mr. POE. Ms. Bigio, if you could be brief, I would appreciate it.

Ms. BIGIO. Thank you.

Right now, the White House has the pen in developing a new national counterterrorism strategy and a new national strategy on countering violent extremist groups.

These should include attention to women as enablers and mitigators of terrorism and it should include a specific objective and focus on these issues.

Second is investment. As the budget is set, women are on the front lines already doing this work and the U.S. Government has done little to support them.

This means ensuring that there are more economic support funds available as well as ensuring that the U.S. Government's security funds, whether antiterrorism or our funds to support police and military, that these pots are also used to support women in the security sector and ensure that they have an opportunity to serve more.

To Mr. Keating's earlier question of the importance of increasing security cooperation efforts to support more female representation in police and military, there are women in the U.S. that—in police that could be training more of their counterparts.

This is a decision in terms of contractors. We should ensure domestically we are leading by example. We are supporting the opportunities for women to serve in the military and police here and that they then have the opportunity to serve—to help train and support their counterparts around the world.

Mr. POE. Thank you. I yield to the ranking member, Mr. Keating, from Massachusetts.

Mr. KEATING. This is a quick round so I will only ask one question.

We've learned, you know, this afternoon how much research— decades of research has been done and how, with our 11 indicators or more—we have more information.

As we get that information, what is our State Department—what is the U.S. Government as well as NGOs doing?

When you're looking at where maybe the next wave of extremism is going to come—countries like Bangladesh, the Philippines, Southeast Asia—we know what's happening there.

It would make great sense to me if we know these indicators and can get information on this. How well are we doing getting—trying to get ahead of the curve a little bit there?

Ms. HUDSON. I am so glad you asked that question because that's the question I've been asking myself.

I received a 4-year $1.3 million grant from the Defense Department to do this research and I am having an awful hard time finding anyone in the Defense Department who would like to actually read this research or listen to this research.

So I am searching for partners within the Defense Department who can take what we've done on the Defense Department's dime and begin to integrate it into intelligence and early warning indicators and also looking at practices, because nations know that they are destabilized by these practices.

For example, the Saudi Government has placed a stiff cap on bride prices and wedding costs in order to prevent these types of inflationary bubbles that occur within their society.

So I think there's a lot more to be done. Now, I know in the State Department we do have the Office of Global Women's Issues.

But my understanding is that their voice has been muted. We do not have a global ambassador for women's issues, which is a serious lack on our part if we are going to take these issues, you know, as importantly as they should be.

So I think there's a lot we need to do. But there's—as you say, we already know a lot. What's missing is the action channels to transfer these knowledge—this knowledge into programs and priorities and funding.

Mr. POE. Thank you.

The chair recognizes the gentleman from Virginia, Mr. Garrett.

Mr. GARRETT. So I want to start out by suggesting that in the year 2018—and I understand that it's not tantamount to purchase, but that any country that institutes any practice that is called bride pricing might be someone who we should consider the nature of our business interaction with regardless of their culture, customs, or tradition.

I mean, it's a head scratcher. I could talk about Saudi Arabia and lots of other countries for a long time and that's not what we are here for.

Mr. Rafiq, I kind of gave you short shrift earlier and I want to give you an opportunity to circle back around. I think my assertion is, however, that in any culture where there's some degree of education and some degree of hope, which is usually provided in conjunction with education, radicalization is less prevalent. I am just going to give you the floor for the balance of my time.

Mr. RAFIQ. Thank you.

I think that if we look at the term radicalization and radicalism, I think radicalism has often been the preserve of the middle class and the educated class.

Whether that's far left radicalization or whether that's far right or whether, in this case, Islam is radicalization.

And the problem that we have—look, I am totally in favor of fixing grievances. I am totally in favor of people becoming more educated because I think that can help civil society as a whole and can be a—help to build more resilient communities against a whole range of problems.

But if we just focus on the grievance culture—if we just focus on the grievances—if we just focus on just the education side of it, well, the four of us here probably have our own personal grievances at this very moment in time.

We can sleep tonight in our own beds. We'll probably have problems and my problem to me will be bigger than somebody else's problem and then tomorrow my problem might be something else, et cetera.

I think that if we just focus on the grievances, we are going to be playing Whac-A-Mole. We should, as a civil society, educate people more because it will help.

We should focus on grievances as a civil society but if we don't focus on the ideology—we don't focus on Islamism, and the—and reverse engineer the intellectual, the ideological, social, emotional, spiritual aspects of Islamism and Salafi jihadism, we won't fix this problem long term, and that's all I was saying.

Mr. GARRETT. So—no, and I think we found some commonality and I will tell you that it strikes me as interesting that we are— you know, I think we are asking Saudi Arabia to revise textbooks that they send literally across the globe while it's not negotiating trillion-dollar arms deals, right.

And I have no problem with—now, I like the Saudis so long as they behave in a manner consistent behind closed doors as they do publicly and that's what makes me shake my head.

And I understand that there are cultural differences and I respect them, and I think that we should respect individuals' rights to live as they choose.

But in the society where individuals don't get to make that choice, I think that the United States foreign policy should be dictated by who we choose to do business with.

It's more efficient than trying to figure out who you need to kill before they kill you.

So thank you, Mr. Chairman, again, for your indulgence and thanks to the members of the panel.

Mr. POE. I thank the gentleman.

The chair recognizes the gentle lady from Florida.

Ms. FRANKEL. Thank you, Mr. Poe.

I think one of the—among other disappointments cf this administration has been the cutting off of health funds to women all over the world, cutting off the funds of the—cutting off the U.S. Population Fund, which I know does work with trafficking and child marriage prevention.

I just—I would be interested in hearing—I should say, on the basis of what I think is a false premise that these organizations and NGOs and so forth are performing abortions, which they're not.

But I would like to hear your opinion on that and in terms of how cutting off so much—so many millions of dollars toward women's health and preventing some of these practices affects terrorism.

Ms. HUDSON. Well, we know that demographic factors absolutely play into terrorism. Researchers have shown that youth bulges especially are associated with internal instability and conflict within nation states.

I have lived long enough to know that women do not wish to have more children than they can take care of. It is when women do not have choice over how many children they have that you get youth bulges.

So I think any policy which reduces women's access to means by which they can control how many children they have is at odds with our desire to see the world be a more peaceful place.

That having been said, I agree with you that while certainly it's a defensible position to say that U.S. funds should not go toward organizations that perform abortions, I can see that.

I think the distinction you made with organizations——

Ms. FRANKEL. Incidentally, that's not my position but that is the position of the United States Government.

Ms. HUDSON. Exactly right.

Ms. FRANKEL. Yes.

Ms. HUDSON. I can see that what you're saying is that there are many organizations that do not perform abortion but nevertheless tell women that abortion is an option and send them off to, you know, to sources where that may be had.

I think that we, you know, probably do have an interest in seeing those organizations succeed. So I agree with you that it is odd that we have cut off money to organizations that don't perform abortions but yet apprise women of means by which to control their fertility.

Ms. BIGIO. Having access to health care is also one of the barriers that prevent women from being able to engage fully in society.

So when they do not have access to the services that they need to ensure their wellbeing and the wellbeing of their families, then this is a barrier, again, to a society being able to draw on its full population to promote prosperity and stability.

So yes, investment in health care, for example, for women and children is part of the full equation to ensure that women and children have the health and opportunity to contribute.

Mr. POE. The gentle lady yields back her time? She does.

Thank you very much, all of you, for being here today. We appreciate it immensely.

This has been one of the better informative hearings that we've had in a long time and I thank you for your time and the information.

All of the members of the subcommittee, even those that were not here, may have questions of you and they will produce those in writing and then we would like a written response on a timely basis, if you will.

I thank you very much. This subcommittee hearing is adjourned.

[Whereupon, at 3:55 p.m., the committee was adjourned.]

APPENDIX

MATERIAL SUBMITTED FOR THE RECORD

SUBCOMMITTEE HEARING NOTICE
COMMITTEE ON FOREIGN AFFAIRS
U.S. HOUSE OF REPRESENTATIVES
WASHINGTON, DC 20515-6128

Subcommittee on Terrorism, Nonproliferation, and Trade
Ted Poe (R-TX), Chairman

TO: MEMBERS OF THE COMMITTEE ON FOREIGN AFFAIRS

You are respectfully requested to attend an OPEN hearing of the Committee on Foreign Affairs, to be held by the Subcommittee on Terrorism, Nonproliferation, and Trade in Room 2172 of the Rayburn House Office Building (and available live on the Committee website at http://www.ForeignAffairs.house.gov):

DATE: Tuesday, February 27, 2018

TIME: 2:00 p.m.

SUBJECT: Women's Role in Countering Terrorism

WITNESSES: Valerie M. Hudson, Ph.D.
Professor and George H.W. Bush Chair
The Bush School of Government and Public Service
Texas A&M University

Mr. Haras Rafiq
Chief Executive Officer
Quilliam International

Ms. Farhat Popal
Manager
Women's Initiative
George W. Bush Institute

Ms. Jamille Bigio
Senior Fellow for Women and Foreign Policy
Council on Foreign Relations

By Direction of the Chairman

COMMITTEE ON FOREIGN AFFAIRS

MINUTES OF SUBCOMMITTEE ON _______ *Terrorism, Nonproliferation, and Trade* _______ HEARING

Day __ *Tuesday* __ Date __ *02/27/2018* __ Room __ *2172* __

Starting Time __ *2:30pm* __ Ending Time __ *3:55pm* __

Recesses ____ (____ to ____) (____ to ____) (____ to ____) (____ to ____) (____ to ____) (____ to ____)

Presiding Member(s)

Representative Poe

Check all of the following that apply:

Open Session ☑
Executive (closed) Session ☐
Televised ☐

Electronically Recorded (taped) ☑
Stenographic Record ☑

TITLE OF HEARING:

"Women's Role in Countering Terrorism"

SUBCOMMITTEE MEMBERS PRESENT:

Rep. Poe, Keating, Zeldin, Frankel, Garrett, Schneider

NON-SUBCOMMITTEE MEMBERS PRESENT: *(Mark with an * if they are not members of full committee.)*

HEARING WITNESSES: Same as meeting notice attached? Yes ☑ No ☐
(If "no", please list below and include title, agency, department, or organization.)

STATEMENTS FOR THE RECORD: *(List any statements submitted for the record.)*

TIME SCHEDULED TO RECONVENE __________
or
TIME ADJOURNED __ *3:55pm* __

Subcommittee Staff Associate